FRED R. VON DER MEHDEN, a specialist in the problems of the developing world, is author of *Religion and Nationalism in Southeast Asia,* co-author of *Issues of Political Development,* and a frequent contributor to professional journals. He was awarded a University of Wisconsin–Ford Foundation grant for research in Southeast Asia in 1963 and was part of a research team assessing American foreign aid in Thailand from 1965 to 1967. Earlier, he conducted research in Burma under a Fulbright award. Dr. von der Mehden received his Ph.D. from the University of California, Berkeley. He currently holds the Albert Thomas Chair in Political Science at Rice University.

POLITICS

OF THE

DEVELOPING

NATIONS

FRED R. VON DER MEHDEN

Prentice-Hall, Inc. A SPECTRUM BOOK *Englewood Cliffs, N. J.*

Current printing (last number):
10 9 8 7 6 5 4 3 2 1

PRENTICE-HALL INTERNATIONAL, INC. (*London*)
PRENTICE-HALL OF AUSTRALIA, PTY. LTD. (SYDNEY)
PRENTICE-HALL OF CANADA, LTD. (*Toronto*)
PRENTICE-HALL OF INDIA PRIVATE LIMITED (*New Delhi*)
PRENTICE-HALL OF JAPAN, INC. (*Tokyo*)

To Audrey, Tori, and Laura

Acknowledgments

A number of people and institutions have been helpful to me in making this study. Special thanks go to David Gugin who collected many of the research materials. I also wish to acknowledge the helpful criticism of my colleagues (particularly Professor Anderson) and my seminar students at the University of Wisconsin and Rice University. For several years, the students in the course entitled "Politics of Underdeveloped Areas" have discussed many of the problems set forth in this book and have thus helped me to crystallize my own thinking on these problems. The University of Wisconsin Research Committee very graciously supplied me with financial aid and research assistance, both of which are greatly appreciated. Finally, thanks must go to the Prentice-Hall editors for their encouragement and for having to deal with a wandering author some 12,000 miles from home.

Chapter VI was originally written in collaboration with Charles Anderson and appeared in the Winter, 1962, issue of *Social Research*. It has been revised for this edition. A short section of Chapter IV appeared in an article in the June 1959 issue of *Social Science*.

F. R. von der M.

CONTENTS

I INTRODUCTION, 1

II THE COLONIAL HERITAGE, 10

III THE SEARCH FOR NATIONAL IDENTITY, 28

IV POLITICAL PARTIES
IN THE DEVELOPING NATIONS, 49

V POLITICAL ELITES
IN THE DEVELOPING NATIONS, 72

POLITICS
OF THE
DEVELOPING
NATIONS

I

INTRODUCTION

The turbulent years of anticolonialist struggle are almost at an end. Except for strategic military bases or entrepôt ports such as Macao, Timor, and Hong Kong, there were no foreign colonies left in Asia by the end of 1963. In Africa only a handful of colonies, primarily Portuguese territories, remain. With the decline of colonialism in its most obvious forms has also come the end of many of the cherished dreams held by political optimists at the end of World War II. The hope that colonial government would be replaced by free democracies has not been fulfilled; instead, one party or a military junta dominates the political scene in the majority of the former colonies. Instead of the hoped-for cooperation between the newly independent states and the West there has arisen a highly emotional nationalism and a strong anti-imperialist feeling directed chiefly toward the former colonial powers. Rather than the peaceful progress toward stable political institutions, the developing nations are experiencing a rash of coups and attempted coups.

The two major problems of the emerging nations have been the maintenance of stable government and the establishment of a unified state. Of the approximately one hundred countries considered in this study, almost two-thirds have been victims of successful coups or serious attempts to overthrow the established governments. Fourteen former colonies achieved independence in the period 1945–55; in eleven of these, the governments have been either attacked or overthrown by extralegal forces. In Afro-Asia alone, twenty-six states have experienced extraconstitutional governments. The figures are not such as to give the early optimists much comfort.

Nor will an analysis of the second problem—that of political disunity—prove more hopeful. In South-Southeast Asia, the former colonial area with the longest history of political independence, not a single country has escaped the problem of dissident groups. Pakistan has her frontier peoples; Ceylon, the Tamil-Sinhalese conflict; Burma, her hill peoples; Thailand, her Chinese and southern Malays; Laos, the non-Mekong Lao; Cambodia, the Vietnamese; Vietnam, the Cambodians and other ethnic and religious groups; Malaysia, a delicate balance among Malays, Chinese, and Indians; while India, the Philippines, and Indonesia must cope with a multitude of different ethnic, language, and religious groups. In many Middle Eastern countries, tensions have arisen over alienated groups such as the Kurds, the Armenians, and various Muslim sects. In Africa, many of the new states are torn by tribal rivalries.

The reaction of the political leaders of these countries has been a continual emphasis upon unity, national loyalty, and the symbols of independence and the state. Divisive influences are considered a mortal danger to the state and these may sometimes include opposition political parties, local and regional parochialism, a free press, and political disengagement. In the new states of Afro-Asia, where the governments attempt to counter instability and disunity by enlisting the entire population in the nation-building crusade, it is becoming increasingly difficult for any individual to remain politically aloof.

The chapters that follow analyze some of the problems of political instability and disunity in the new nations. To provide a setting for this analysis, Chapter I examines the economic, social, and political heritage of colonialism. Chapter II considers the basic problem of national identity as well as forms of alienation and efforts to counter their impact on the developing countries. The rest of the book surveys the present status of political parties, elites, and national ideologies as they touch upon the twin issues of unity and stability. A final chapter attempts to draw attention to important political trends in the areas under consideration.

The study of developing countries must be viewed against the background of postwar analyses of the nature of the "underdeveloped" state which, before World War II, were dominated by historical, administrative, and anthropological studies.

Until recently the political scientist found, then, a set of readymade models of underdeveloped countries, but these models were prepared by economists, sociologists, and historians. Thus, he was provided with definitions which may or may not be politically relevant. Economists and sociologists, for instance, use such criteria as per capita income, industrialization and literacy rates, and the like as bases for identifying an underdeveloped area.

Furthermore, the average American has built a stereotype of an "underdeveloped" country. According to this stereotype, a state is considered underdeveloped if it cannot be related to a model based upon a Western European or North American polity which is democratic and which has several political parties, widespread literacy, a high standard of living, wide circulation of newspapers and books, consensus on the fundamentals of government, a long history of peace, and (in some models) a white population.

There is need for considerable analysis by political scientists to discover acceptable definitions of political underdevelopment or, at least, to loosen the shackles imposed by current definitions. The two primary problems are those of value and information. First, almost all descriptions of political development have been value-laden: comparisons between Latin America or Afro-Asia and the "developed" world have been based on Western norms. A second problem arises from an insufficient knowledge of the nature of the political process in the developing world, which has all too often led to unrealistic conclusions.

There are three cogent reasons for considering the problem of the politically underdeveloped state. There is the intriguing question of whether or not economic and social factors are related to political development. S. Lipset, for example, suggests that nations with high indices of education, urbanization, industrialization, and wealth tend to be stable and democratic. The same conclusion is implied by other writers in this field. J. Coleman, using Lipset's materials, has explored his hypothesis that "there is a positive correlation between economic development and political competitiveness." These men present challenging theories; but whether democracy, stability, or political competitiveness should be criteria for political development is, of course, another question—and one that needs further consideration.

A second reason for the study of political development is that such a study may diminish the tendency to view all underdeveloped areas as one. Serious mistakes can be made by those who assume that a similarity in social and economic standards indicates a similarity in political development. Far too often overly generalized terms are applied to areas that differ markedly from one another.

Third, the definition of *underdeveloped areas* leads to a host of interesting questions of political theory and comparative government. Questions of political theory may be dealt with by employing the tools of analysis found useful by political theorists in the past. Questions of comparative government, on the other hand, require a comparative evaluation of various criteria for political development. If a definition of political underdevelopment rests on such criteria as government instability, the presence of serious anomic disturbances, and the absence of civil liberties, how then is France to be classified? If Western democratic values are presumed, how is the Soviet Union to be classified? And is Czechoslovakia to be described as having swung from political underdevelopment (as part of Austria-Hungary) to political development (the interwar period) to underdevelopment (under Hitler) to development (1945–48) to underdevelopment (under Communist rule) and then back toward development prior to the Soviet-led invasion of 1968? The problems presented by the selection of criteria are both complex and challenging for the student of politics who attempts to compare different political systems.

These reasons for analysis give rise to another question: How has the problem of definition been approached in the past and what have been the problems attendant on each approach? The four most prominent approaches have been based, respectively, on general normative goals, relativism, a set of specific criteria which must be met in whole or in part, or the concept of a historical continuum.

Normative definitions of political development are both proudly propounded and unconsciously implied. It is not unusual to find Western politicians and scholars using Western systems of government as the criterion for political development or "modernity." The idea that "a democratic system is only to be found in advanced states" or that a particular country is not "ready" for democracy is commonly expressed by politicians and journalists in the West. The assumption that democracy and "modernity"—defined according to Western values—are essential to development is implicit in most studies of the politics of developing areas. For example, Martin Needler's article on Mexico notes the development from the "vicious circle of dictatorship, misery, and revolution" to a system that is developed, stable, and democratic.[1]

These value-laden definitions are sharply criticized by many Afro-Asian politicians and writers, who claim that many Western values may not be relevant to their nations. In the words of K. H. Pfeffer of the University of Punjab:

> The term "under-developed" country is based on the assumption that there exists a commonly accepted standard of development. A person or

[1] "The Political Development of Mexico," *APSR*, 55 (June 1961), 308–13.

a group or a nation can only be called under-developed when there is general agreement what a developed or a fully developed person, nation, or group ought to be like. Thus, the very category "under-developed" should be tested before it is thoughtlessly used. The category itself is loaded with values and prejudices.[2]

Orthodox Marxists have been even more articulate in their discussions of development within their system of dialectics. Obviously, according to their theories, a feudal state is less developed than one with an established bourgeoisie, and both are less developed than one that has achieved socialism. But in spite of Marxist assertions that theirs is a scientific system (and without arguing the point that the support of science itself may be a normative position), most Western observers would describe Marxian goals as normative in nature.

Most prominent, however, has been the discussion of the twin goals of modernity and democracy, each of which is based upon values of the Western industrial revolution. Not all of these values are necessarily acceptable to adherents of relativism, including some Afro-Asian politicians and Western writers (particularly anthropologists) who regard given goals and definitions as valid only within particular societies. Most political leaders in the Afro-Asian world reject Western competitive democracy, preferring to find their political ideals within their own societies. (See Chapter VII.) A similar rejection of Western values appears to occur among anthropologists; but it is a rare political scientist who would define political development in terms of locally established goals. Indeed, until recently, there has been a certain blindness to the very existence of such parochial attitudes.[3]

The third definition of development involves a variety of factors which must be met in whole or in part. These points, again, usually reflect Western values. This system, however, gives rise to serious problems concerning the number and the nature of the factors to be included, and the relative importance of each. A list of possible factors is presented below. These factors are not arranged in order of importance or significance; they are intended only to illustrate the variety of criteria which might be considered.

1. A national consensus on basic social and political goals.
2. Communication between the leaders and the masses.

[2] "Is Pakistan an Underdeveloped Country?" *Pakistan Today* (1960), p. 28.
[3] At least one political theorist has recently argued that the acceptance of democracy as a system does not tie the society to any one set of goals. The argument is that democracy provides the framework for the achievement of aims decided upon by the community. See T. Thorson, *Logic of Democracy* (New York: Holt, Rinehart & Winston, Inc., 1962).

3. The national integration of minority groups.
4. The secularization of politics.
5. High literacy rates.
6. A sizable group which has achieved higher education.
7. A trained civil service.
8. A competitive political system.
9. Political institutions with specific and differentiated functions.
10. Political activity which is widespread, rather than confined to the capital city.
11. The infusion of Western political and social values into the system.
12. The existence of associational interest groups.
13. The possibility of political mobility.
14. The existence of constitutional government in its broadest context, and the absence of major anomic disturbances.
15. Civilian control of the military.

Other criteria might be included, but those who suggest this approach would identify a politically developed area by the extent to which the country in question meets all or some of the goals given here. It is possible to give some of these criteria added emphasis, or to select only a few which must be achieved. If all the goals given above are used as the standard of political development, in the Afro-Asian area only Japan and Israel could meet the definition—with the Philippines, India, and Malaysia only approaching it. Again, it should be noted that these criteria are based on Western values and that this method of describing political underdevelopment is only a variation on the first system.

Another method of defining political underdevelopment has been to view the states in question in relation to the historical development of a "developed" state, such as the United States or the United Kingdom. The United States, for example, might be considered to have been new and underdeveloped in the eighteenth century, unified by 1865, industrialized by 1914, and so on. According to this standard, Indonesia's level of development would be comparable to ours in 1775–85; India's level of development might be comparable to ours in, say, the mid-nineteenth century. Given the swift growth possible during the twentieth century, it is not necessary for a state to be as old as the United States in order to approach its level of development. Yet other states—Ethiopia, for instance—may be much older but much less developed. The ethnocentricity of this approach is obvious, although it does open the mind to some fascinating analogies.

None of these approaches is wholly satisfactory; any one may be considered to be value-laden or invidious by the sensitive Afro-Asians. Even the simple description of material differences between the West and Afro-Asia may be resented as not giving proper consideration to cultural differences between the two. Yet the underdeveloped world is discussed as an economic and political entity and, as such, merits attention.

Two avenues of speculation have been considered in this book. The entire area of Latin America, Africa, and Asia (the regions usually termed *underdeveloped* by economists and politicians) has been surveyed in an effort to ascertain if, in fact, it has characteristic political processes. The political usefulness of the term *underdeveloped*, as used by other disciplines, can then be tested. After this area has been examined on several levels, it may be possible to define more accurately the boundaries of the problem.

Or, it may be possible to agree upon the lowest common denominator of political underdevelopment. For instance, few would describe as politically developed a state that is unable to provide for its citizens both physical safety and the necessities of life (enough food to prevent starvation and sufficient housing to stop exposure).

No effort has been made to provide a comprehensive analysis of each new country. Instead, the general outlines of the problems are presented, together with illustrations and examples.

The evidence upon which these analyses are based are necessarily somewhat less than conclusive. There are few political studies of individual Afro-Asian countries comparable to D. Apter's book on Uganda, J. Coleman's study of Nigeria, or H. Feith's work on Indonesia. Even more rare are detailed analyses of national elites or political parties and ideologies in these countries. Even the governments of the new nations are often less than eager to provide the simplest statistics on voting and parliamentary procedures—particularly when elections have been held under questionable conditions. The statistics furnished in other categories are often suspect, too. One government official admitted to the author that literacy rates in his country were lower than they had been during the colonial period; his government had given the United Nations artificially high figures, he explained, because of national pride.

Finally, these analyses cannot be entirely accurate because they deal with situations in flux. Although the basic patterns appear to remain fairly constant, their elements—the party in power, the dominant ideology, and even the composition of the national elite—may not be the same from one year to the next. The very instability which is under analysis must be taken into account when the charts and examples are considered. These changes, however, take place within what has become a general pattern, and change itself is part of that pattern.

SELECTED BIBLIOGRAPHY

Almond, G. and J. Coleman, *The Politics of the Developing Areas.* Princeton, N. J.: Princeton University Press, 1960.

———— and G. Powell, *Comparative Politics: A Developmental Approach.* Boston: Little, Brown & Co., 1966.

Apter, D., *Some Conceptual Approaches to the Study of Modernization.* Englewood Cliffs, N. J.: Prentice-Hall, Inc., 1968.

Eckstein, H., *A Theory of Stable Democracy.* Princeton, N. J.: Center of International Studies, Princeton University, 1961.

Holt, R. and J. Turner, *The Political Basis of Economic Development.* Princeton, N. J.: D. Van Nostrand Co., Inc., 1966.

Huntington, S., *Political Order in Changing Societies.* New Haven, Conn.: Yale University Press, 1968.

Lipset, S. M., *Political Man.* Garden City, N. Y.: Doubleday & Company, Inc., 1960.

McClelland, D., *The Achieving Society.* Princeton, N. J.: D. Van Nostrand Co., Inc., 1961.

Millikan, M. and D. Blackmer, *The Emerging Nations.* Boston: Little, Brown & Co., 1961.

Organski, A., *The Stages of Political Development.* New York: Alfred A. Knopf, 1965.

Pye, L., *Politics, Personality and Nation Building.* New Haven, Conn.: Yale University Press, 1962.

Rostow, W. W., *The Stages of Economic Growth.* London: Cambridge University Press, 1960.

Shannon, L., *Underdeveloped Areas.* New York: Harper & Row, Publishers, 1957.

Staley, E., *The Future of Underdeveloped Countries.* New York: Harper & Row, Publishers, 1954.

Ward, B., *The Rich Nations and the Poor Nations*. New York: W. W. Norton & Company, Inc., 1962.

Welch, C., ed., *Political Modernization*. Belmont, Calif.: Wadsworth Publishing Co., 1967.

II

The Colonial Heritage

Discussion of the impact of colonialism on the controlled territories usually elicits a variety of highly emotional responses. Even those Afro-Asians who recognize the material benefits brought about by the European occupation are quick to add, as did Guinea's Sekou Touré: "But the happiness of man does not come merely from material things." Therefore, any analysis of the objective material benefits of colonialism must take into account the subjective reactions of a people to foreign domination. Yet such an analysis is worth consideration—at least as a partial summation of one phase of the experiences of the developing world.

A number of contemporary writers have listed, as the key changes brought about by colonial administrations, the establishment and maintenance of order; the provision of at least a minimum of national unity through the maintenance of stable institutions, education and communication; and the introduction of institutions and processes new to the area. The profoundness of these changes is open to considerable debate. Some observers of the African scene, such as I. Wallerstein, strongly emphasize the importance of the precolonial period and the relative brevity of colonial rule. Others, such as Roland Young, insist on the more powerful influence of European rule.

To deal with this problem, we must ask and attempt to answer several questions: What, if any, have been the differences in material progress between those states which remained independent and those which were subjected to European domination? What varieties of social and economic progress have been experienced among the colonial powers themselves? Is it possible to draw any conclusions as to the political heritage of different types of colonial rule—particularly with regard to the preparation of the colony for stable, unified self-government?

To answer these questions, colonial and noncolonial states, as well as different types of colonial administration, must be compared on two points: the objective economic and social factors that prevailed near the time of independence, and the political system established after independence.

This approach obviously has several attendant problems. A comparison of colonial and noncolonial states must take into account the fact that no African or Asian country was completely isolated from European influences or imperialist pressures. A number of states, notably Japan and Thailand, initiated reforms precisely in order to remain out of the clutches of the imperial powers. Some states were independent in name only, for much of their internal administration and foreign relations were under European control. A second problem centers on the fact that we are comparing areas whose resources, precolonial histories, and—in some cases—demographic patterns differ. An effort has been made to compare only those areas which are geographically similar. Finally, those states which remained independent were often poor in resources or off normal trade routes—facts which may put such states at a disadvantage in comparisons with richer colonial states. Nevertheless, a general pattern does emerge which covers a variety of historic and economic differences.

COLONIES AND NONCOLONIES COMPARED

Colonial and noncolonial systems. One way of assessing the impact of colonial rule is to compare those states which remained independent with those of their neighbors which fell under foreign control. One nation from each major geographical area has been chosen for comparison with its neighbors: from West Africa, Liberia (her neighbors: former French and British colonies); from East Africa, Ethiopia (her neighbors: former British East Africa, Somalia, and Sudan); from Southeast Asia, Thailand (her neighbors: Burma, Laos, Cambodia, Vietnam, and Malaya); from East Asia, Japan (her neighbors: the Philippines, Korea, and China). These states will be compared on the basis of education, newspaper circulation, agriculture and urbanization, food consumption, and nonhuman energy consumption.

1. EDUCATION. Major variations in education exist in Asia and Africa. In Asia, Japan and Thailand have for decades maintained major programs of education. Both have a higher literacy rate and a larger percentage of total population in secondary and higher educa-

tion than do their neighbors. Indeed, Japan has one of the highest literacy rates in the world. Almost the opposite is true in Africa, where the traditionally independent states—Liberia and Ethiopia—are each

Chart 2-1. Literacy Rates Among Adults (%)

Liberia	5–10	Ethiopia	1–5*
French West Africa	5–10	Somalia	1–5
British West Africa	5–25	Sudan	5–10
		Kenya	20–25
		Uganda	25–30
Thailand	50–55	Japan	97–98
French Indo-China	15–20	Korea	35–40
Malaya	35–40	China	45–50*
Burma	55–60*	Philippines	60–65

* Accuracy suspect.

at or below the level of their neighbors in these categories. The world mean for postprimary education is 2.29 per cent of the population. As Chart 2-2 indicates, Ethiopia has a mean of 0.02 per cent while Liberia has one of 0.11 per cent.[1]

Chart 2-2. Percentage of Total Population in Postprimary School*

Liberia	0.11	Ethiopia	0.02
French West Africa	0.10	Somalia	0.11
British West Africa	0.27–0.34	Sudan	0.09
		Kenya	0.21
		Uganda	0.37
Thailand	1.56	Japan	5.64
French Indo-China	0.40	Korea	3.24
Malaya	1.42	China	0.77
Burma	1.06	Philippines	3.98

* West Germany has the highest percentage: 7.34; the United States percentage is 6.02.

2. NEWSPAPER CIRCULATION. Newspapers are of major use in disseminating ideas and providing communication. Newspaper circulation in Japan is very high—far outstripping that of every country in Asia

[1] N. Ginsburg, *Atlas of Economic Development* (Chicago: University of Chicago Press, 1961). Statistics from this chapter have been derived primarily from Ginsburg and from United Nations figures. Dates of compilation were approximately at the time of independence of the new states.

and, in fact, most of the world. Thailand, Liberia, and Ethiopia have a lower rate of newspaper circulation than their neighbors. (It should be pointed out that no nation in Southeast Asia or East or West Africa has a very high newspaper circulation rate and that daily newspapers are largely lacking in the rural areas of these regions.)

3. AGRICULTURE AND URBANIZATION. Economic progress has usually been concomitant to a specialization of skills and urban development. The world mean is 59 per cent of the population active in agriculture. Of the four states under consideration here, all but Japan have means well above the world figure and, generally, above those of their neighbors. In urbanization (that is, the percentage of the population living in cities of over 100,000), Japan again ranks high, while the other three states fall below most of their former colonial neighbors. Ethiopia has 2.6 per cent urbanization (only Somalia and Tanganyika have lower percentages); Thailand, 4.5 per cent (only Cambodia has a lower percentage); and Liberia, 0 per cent (along with Sierra Leone and Togo).

4. FOOD CONSUMPTION. The daily per capita calory intake is one criterion of how well the economic system works, though obviously the resources available and the types of food eaten are also significant. Japan, Thailand, and Liberia are all less well off than most of their neighbors in this respect.

5. NONHUMAN ENERGY CONSUMPTION. Closely related to industrialization are the rates of electric generation and commercial energy consumption. The rates of Ethiopia and Thailand fall well below those of their neighbors and are comparable to those of Liberia; Japan's rates, however, are higher than those of her neighbors.

What do these figures reveal about the heritage of colonialism? Very generally, Japan is the only traditionally independent state which has been able to provide social and economic benefits higher than those of her foreign-dominated neighbors. In fact, Japan is the only Afro-Asian state which ranks in the top two-fifths of the countries of the world in technology; all the other continually independent states rank in the bottom one-fifth. For these others, there appears to have been no material advantage in independence; in fact, just the opposite may be said to have been the case. Norton Ginsburg, in his *Atlas of Economic Development,* has established a demographic scale which considers birth and death rates, infant mortality rates, population growth, population density, population per unit of cultivated land, rice yield per hectare, trade statistics, newspaper circulation per capita, gross national product, and number of telephones and automobiles. He is considering, then, "essentially a demographic scale revealing similar-

ities in the population characteristics and well-being of countries,"
and, he concludes:

> Colonies and ex-colonies fare "better" demographically than otherwise
> independent countries. . . . The fact that colonialism, or at least political
> colonialism, seems not to explain poverty but even in some instances to
> have countered it, is at variance with the assumptions of perhaps three
> fourths of the world.[2]

Nor can it be argued that a tradition of independence provides a
better atmosphere for learning the Western democratic system. Liberia,
for instance, is a one-party state which has in the past provided few
rights to noncoastal groups. Ethiopia is one of the last absolute monar-
chies left in the world. Thailand is dominated by the military. Japan
has achieved a tenuous democracy only for short periods in its history.

Few of their neighbors did any better, however. Again, the methodological problems attendant on this approach and the few cases
with which we have dealt make this analysis somewhat suspect. We
can only expect that it will supply some clues to the relationship between independence and material progress. The general answer would
appear to be that there is no necessary correlation between them.

COLONIAL SYSTEMS COMPARED

The heritage of the colonial systems. A variety of arguments have
been forwarded as to the merits of one colonial system over another.
Francophiles point to the assimilation of races and the instillation of
"French" civilization in their former territories; Anglophiles point to
the transfer of British institutions and systems of education; the Portuguese point to the transplantation of "Catholic Portuguese" civilization and order; and the Belgians point to the higher literacy rates and
more advanced technical skills to be found among their former colonial subjects.

We will compare the heritages of the colonial systems in the various
geographic regions—sub-Sahara Africa (excluding the Central African
Federation and the Union of South Africa), Southeast Asia, the Middle East, and Latin America—in the areas of education, communications, and industrialization.

1. EDUCATION. The colonial heritage in education should be viewed
on two levels: literacy and postprimary education. Literacy is the bare

[2] *Ibid.*, pp. 113–19 (Italics are Ginsburg's).

minimum required in order to act effectively in a Western environment. Postprimary education is essential for political and economic
development. Literacy figures, which are always highly suspect, appear
in Chart 2-3. They are based on the median of former colonies in each
region.

Chart 2-3.   Literacy Rates among Adults in Former Colonial Areas (%)

Colonial Power	Southeast Asia	Africa	Middle East
United States	50		
United Kingdom	35–40	10–15	10–15
France	15–20	1–5	15–20
Netherlands	10–15		
Belgium		35–40	
Portugal		1–5	

All these former colonial areas had literacy rates lower than Latin
America's mean of 50–55 per cent—many, far lower. There is little to
distinguish among the efforts of the various colonial systems—although
of the major colonial powers, the United Kingdom was somewhat more
effective than France and certainly far more so than Portugal.

Of far greater importance is postprimary education, which usually
provides the basis for efficient self-rule. In few former colonies do postprimary education figures even approach the world mean. Again, the
percentages are very small and the differences in percentile points
among areas is minimal. Nor do the figures show either the type of
postprimary education received or its duration. For example, the education provided in Belgium's colonies was almost entirely technical;
universities were established in these territories only a few years prior
to independence. On the other hand, the British had for decades made
available a broader type of education in Asia.

Chart 2-4.   Percentage of Population with Postprimary Education*

Colonial Power	Southeast Asia	Africa	Middle East
United States	3.98		
United Kingdom	1.06	0.24	1.05
France	0.13	0.15	1.31
Netherlands	0.65		
Belgium		0.22	
Portugal		0.08	

* Latin America: 1.0.

2. COMMUNICATIONS. Transportation and communication systems are usually necessary in establishing unity and aiding economic development in new nations. Rail and road densities and newspaper circulation rates provide some indices of the level of communication within a country. The significance of such figures, however, is not clear unless differences in population and area are also taken into account.

Chart 2-5.   Kilometers of Railroad Per 100,000 Inhabitants*

Colonial Power	Southeast Asia	Africa	Middle East
United States	4.2		
United Kingdom	15.0	27.0	14.0
France	7.9	36.0	18.0
Netherlands	7.7		
Belgium		47.0	
Portugal		35.0	

* Latin America: 33.0.

Chart 2-6.   Kilometers of Road Per 100 Square Kilometers of Area

Colonial Power	Southeast Asia	Africa	Middle East
United States	9.9		
United Kingdom	8.0	6.0	1.6
France	3.7	2.4	5.5
Netherlands	3.2		
Belgium		1.7	
Portugal		4.7	

Chart 2-7.   Newspaper Circulation Per 1000 Inhabitants*

Colonial Power	Southeast Asia	Africa	Middle East
United States	19.0		
United Kingdom	22.0	6.0	10.0
France		1.0	22.0
Netherlands	11.0		
Belgium		2.0	
Portugal		1.9	

* Latin America: 33.0.

3. INDUSTRIALIZATION. Demands for industrialization by new nations can be viewed in the light of the heritage of steel and energy consumption established by the various colonial governments.

Chart 2-8.   Steel Consumption: 100 Metric Tons Per 1000 Inhabitants*

Colonial Power	Southeast Asia	Africa	Middle East
United States	12.7		
United Kingdom	6.1	3.6	14.7
France	2.1	4.2	24.0
Netherlands	3.3		
Belgium		13.0	
Portugal		2.5	

* Latin America: 14.0.

Chart 2-9.   Gross Electrical Energy Consumption Per Capita*

Colonial Power	Southeast Asia	Africa	Middle East
United States	1.2		
United Kingdom	1.0	0.4	0.8
France	0.3	0.2	1.6
Netherlands	0.8		
Belgium		1.3	
Portugal		0.45	

* Latin America: 2.6.

Still another index of economic well-being is the per capita gross national product, which is closely tied to problems of resource patterns, income distribution, and exchange rates. There is also the problem of assessing the dollar value of the gross national product of subsistence-level agricultural societies. Nevertheless, some general patterns can be discerned.[3]

Per Capita Budgeting Revenue for 1956

British Colonies		French Colonies		Others	
Ghana	$29.4	West Africa	$15.7	Belgian Congo	$13.4
Kenya	16.0	Cameroon	14.8	Liberia	10.0
Gambia	14.0	Equatorial Africa	10.4		
Sierra Leone	12.9	Togo	6.4		
Uganda	9.0				
Nigeria	7.8				
Tanganyika	6.7				

[3] Another method of viewing this factor would be to look at the per capita budgeting revenue. The following is a selected list taken from G. Kimble, *Tropical Africa* (New York: Twentieth Century Fund, 1960), II, 355.

Chart 2-10.   Gross National Product Per Capita*

Colonial Power	Southeast Asia	Africa	Middle East
United States	$201		
United Kingdom	72	$70	$100
France	133	58	159
Netherlands	127		
Belgium		98	
Portugal		70	

* Latin America: $244.

There are no striking differences among the different colonial systems in these statistics. Generally, the distribution of material benefits may be said to be highest in territories formerly controlled by the United States, with those formerly controlled by Belgium, United Kingdom, Netherlands, France, and Portugal following in that order. However, the differences are so small that it cannot be argued that any one colonial system (with the possible exception of the United States, a rich country with few colonies) has provided a consistently better economic and social order for its possessions. Also, the resource pattern in a given area is often as important as the colonial system in determining economic levels, and these—in turn—influence the social benefits that can be attained. However, since the variations in resource patterns among the areas under consideration are far sharper than differences in gross national product, it is clear that colonial policy must bear some responsibility for the economic levels attained by the newly independent nations.

COLONIAL POLITICAL MODELS REJECTED

Political institutions and processes are not shaped by colonial administration alone; nevertheless, general patterns have emerged under the different colonial systems. Two factors are significant: the level of political stability, as based upon the number of revolutions or major coups (whether successful or not) to which the new nation has been subjected; and the type of government established after independence, on the basis of party system and extraconstitutional control of the government (primarily military takeover or suspension of democratic institutions).

1. ATTEMPTED REVOLUTIONS AND COUPS.

Chart 2-11. Postcolonial Revolutions and Coup Attempts in Afro-Asia

Colonial Power	Number of Colonies	Number of Former Colonies Subjected to Revolutions or Coup Attempts
France	24	16 (67%)[1]
United Kingdom	24	15 (62%)[2]
Belgium	3	3 (100%)[3]
United States	1	1 (100%)[4]
Netherlands	1	1 (100%)[5]
Independent States	11	10 (91%)[6]

[1] Laos, South Vietnam, Syria, Lebanon, Senegal, Algeria, Togo, Dahomey, Mali, Cambodia, Central African Republic, Congo, Gabon, Morocco, Tunisia, Upper Volta

[2] Nigeria, Pakistan, Ceylon, Burma, Iraq, Jordan, Sudan, Tanzania (Zanzibar), Ghana, Kenya, Sierra Leone, Uganda, Singapore, Guyana

[3] Congo, Rwanda, Burundi

[4] Philippines

[5] Indonesia

[6] Thailand, Turkey, Liberia, Saudi Arabia, Yemen, Ethiopia, China, Korea, Iran, Egypt. Only those states which have been independent during the twentieth century are considered. Arabian sheikdoms and Himalayan kingdoms are not considered. Their inclusion would vastly increase the number of states with revolts, attempted and successful.

Several interesting points appear in this chart. Instability, as defined by the incidence of attempted or successful coups or revolution, can be correlated to the length of time a country has been independent. It should be noted that former British colonies, which show a higher percentage of instability, have been independent longer than most French colonies and thus have had more time in which to develop internal troubles. (Also, a number of those areas experiencing revolutions and coups—Lebanon, Syria, Iraq, Togo, and Jordan—were not colonies but were administered as mandates.) Only Liberia has not displayed this common tendency in recent years. One method of testing this correlation between time and instability might be to compare the level of stability in former colonies and mandates which have achieved their independence before 1958 with that of those which received theirs later.

These figures show an almost universal instability among countries which achieved independence before 1958. Perhaps it would not be unfair to conclude that if the former colonial administrators intended

Chart 2-12. Attempted Coups and Revolutions in Former Colonies
Independent Before 1958

Colonial Power	Number of Colonies	Number with Coups and Revolutions
France	8	8
United Kingdom	7	6*
Netherlands	1	1
United States	1	1
Total	17	16

* Malaya endured a continuing revolt after independence was achieved.

Chart 2-13. Attempted Coups and Revolutions in Former Colonies
Independent Since 1958 or Later

Colonial Power	Number of Colonies	Number with Coups and Revolutions
France	16	8
United Kingdom	17	7
Belgium	3	3
Total	36	18

to provide the foundations for peace and order, they were somewhat less than successful.

2. POSTINDEPENDENCE SYSTEMS OF GOVERNMENT: AFRO-ASIA. Extraconstitutional governments have also been common in former colonies which have been independent for longer periods of time. Chart 2-14 shows the number and percentage of former colonies and mandates that have had military governments or the suspension of democratic systems.

Chart 2-14. Extraconstitutional Governments in Former Colonies

Colonial Power	Number of Former Colonies with Extraconstitutional Governments*
France	10 (42%)
United Kingdom	10 (42%)
Belgium	2 (67%)
United States	0 (0%)
Netherlands	1 (100%)
Independent States	7 (63%)

* Only states which have become independent since World War II are considered.

Chart 2-15 shows the type of party system established in former colonies after independence. (The system of classification is explained in Chapter IV.)

Chart 2-15. Types of Party Systems Established
in Former Colonies After Independence

Colonial Power	No Effective Party Control	Prole-tariat	One-Party	One-Party Dominant	Two-Party	Multi-party
France	8	1	12	1	0	2
United Kingdom	7	0	1	5	1	4
Belgium	2	0	1	0	0	0
United States	0	0	0	0	1	0
Netherlands	1	0	0	0	0	0

It is one of the ironies of postwar politics that France, often criticized for the instability and *immobilisme* of her multiparty system, should be the mother to so many one-party states. Of the twenty-four former French colonies and mandates now independent, thirteen have one-party dominant systems. The major influence on the politics of former French colonies may have come from the French Left, to which so many postwar African leaders were drawn. The other irony is that the United Kingdom—the "Mother of Parliaments"—has tied France for the largest number of states with extraconstitutional governments and has spawned seven political systems in which parties play no effective role. In fact, of the Afro-Asian governments in which the military has led a successful coup, France and Britain hold equal honors with eight formerly controlled territories each. Again, this instability may arise from the fact that these states have been independent for relatively longer periods. The United States can, perhaps, claim some of the credit for the only independent Afro-Asian country with a democratic two-party system: the Philippines.

In conclusion, it cannot be stated that the colonial powers provided their colonies with the foundations for democratic systems similar to their own. It is almost as though the former colonies had consciously rejected the proffered model.

FAILURES OF COLONIAL TUTELAGE

Why were the colonial governments so remiss in preparing their colonies for stable independence? It is currently the fashion to ascribe the instability of the developing nations to one of two causes: the desire of the capitalist imperialists to keep the former colonial peoples in political and economic servitude, or the international Communist conspiracy. Such simplistic explanations, of course, ignore the deeper causes of instability, the roots of which lie in the type of colonial government established, the manner in which independence was achieved, and the inherent economic and social problems which beset most of the Afro-Asian world.

Colonial administration, with rare exceptions, was poor preparation for self-government. In most cases the period of training in modern administration and the time available to expand communications and to unite dissident groups was extremely short. The average period of colonialism for the African nations was only about seventy-five years. Also, until the twentieth century few colonial powers considered it their duty to prepare their colonies for independence. (Portugal still refuses to admit the idea.) Even after the colonial powers acknowledged their responsibility, numerous obstacles were posed by die-hard colonialists at home and in the field. The degree of "nativization" varied from colony to colony and among the various colonial systems, but many a report on "nativization" of the civil service noted the unwillingness of colonial officers to entrust responsibility to the native peoples. Toward the end of World War II, the French government asked its senior civil servants to provide the names of Africans capable of filling high posts. None was submitted. A British report on the Nigerianization of the civil service commented adversely on the attitude of senior civil servants toward the advancement of Africans to high posts. Where there existed a "proletariat" of lower-rank European civil servants, as in French Indo-China and the Dutch East Indies, the problem was even more difficult and training began even later.

Perhaps the most effective colonial power, in this respect, was the United States, which had largely nativized the civil service of the Philippines by the 1920's. The British also had a good record, although it varied greatly. For example, a comparatively good program was established in India and Ceylon, but nativization began much later in

Chart 2-16.   Africanization of the Gold Coast
Senior Civil Service, 1949-57[4]

Year (as of April)	Foreigners	Africans
1949	1068	171
1951	1200	351
1953	1329	743
1955	1319	1166
1957	1135	1581

[4] Ibid., 355-57.

Ghana, Nigeria, and Uganda, and still later in the former colonies of Somalia, Lesotho, Tanzania, the former Rhodesias, and Malawi.

In Uganda, only five higher civil service posts were occupied by Africans in 1952 and fifty in 1958. It was hoped that one quarter of the higher posts would be Africanized by the time independence was achieved. The pace was so slow that, some claimed, it would take twenty-five years before Uganda was 70 per cent Africanized. Uganda —like so many other states—became independent before her administrators were adequately trained, and personal and political pressures caused the country to lose its trained foreigners. (It was estimated that 60 per cent of the European civil servants left the country by March, 1963.) In an even more difficult position were Tanzania and Malawi. In Tanzania, only 700 of the 4889 senior staff positions had been Africanized by late 1961, at which time there were in Malawi only thirty-three natives educationally trained to take over the more highly skilled posts. It was estimated that if the 1960–61 rate of education in Malawi were maintained, there would be only 120 properly trained personnel to fill these posts by 1971.

The French had achieved a very high percentage of Africanization at the lower levels (almost 100 per cent in West and Equatorial Africa by the mid-1950's), but a much lower percentage in the middle levels (about 25 per cent in West Africa and 33 per cent in Equatorial Africa), and they admitted very few Africans to top-level policymaking positions (perhaps 6 per cent in Equatorial Africa).

The Belgians entrusted no policymaking positions to Africans until the very late 1950's. Native Congolese were almost universally held to clerical positions and could not rise above the rank of noncommissioned officer in the army. (To discuss Africanization in the Spanish and Portuguese colonies would be to give too much space to what has been almost totally nonexistent.)

One aspect of this "too little too late" training was that the post-independence civil service suffered from a paucity of experienced officers at top levels. Where the Europeans refused to cooperate with the new nation (the French took everything—including office fixtures —from Guinea when that country refused to enter the French Community), or where Europeans were dismissed before nationals had been adequately trained (as in Indonesia), serious administrative problems arose. In a number of countries, the problem was further complicated by nationalist charges that the natives who had worked for the colonial civil service were "tools" of the "imperialists" or "antinationalists" and therefore not fit for higher positions. The most obvious examples of this situation occurred in Burma and Indonesia, where the colonial administrators had employed a high percentage of members of religious and ethnic minority groups in civil service positions.

Furthermore, many civil servants who did not suffer from the stigma of colonialism too often preferred to enter politics, leaving serious gaps in both central and provincial administration. (Provincial governments also lost able participants to national politics.) This was more natural in former French colonies, where the civil servant was not expected to remain aloof from politics. Thus, some new countries lost their trained civil service personnel while others—including almost all Afro-Asian states—attained independence with an insufficiently trained staff to back politicians who were often even less experienced.

A second factor of colonialism which led to later instability was the paternalistic attitude of the colonial powers. One commentator on the Dutch administration in the Indies called it a "hothouse atmosphere." This charge could be made against others as well. The philosophy of "the white man's burden" had several serious effects on postcolonial stability and unity. Paternalism did not foster self-reliance in the native population. Even more serious, the postindependence native administrators often retained an aloofness and an air of *noblesse oblige* which was characteristic of the colonial period. A relationship based upon mutual trust and respect could not develop and too little consideration was given to popular beliefs by those who thought that they knew what was "best" for the people.

The practice of indirect rule, the unwillingness in certain cases to expand the use of the colonial or national language, and the disproportionate use of minority groups in government posts all led to post-independence conflicts and difficulties in communication which complicated efforts to establish stable government. In some areas, as in French West Africa, the colonial regime had replaced traditional local rulers with bureaucrats who could not command the traditional respect and authority based on local tribal, religious, or blood ties. To a certain extent, the colonial authorities were damned if they did maintain traditional rule (thus perpetuating parochial loyalties) and damned if they didn't.

Finally, the economic systems established by the colonial governments left the Afro-Asian states at the mercy of the world primary market economy—although it can be argued that this was inevitable. In their efforts to derive economic benefits from their colonies while raising the standard of living in these areas, the colonial powers encouraged the development of economies based upon the export of such products as rubber, tin, cocoa, peanuts, coffee, sugar, rice, and spices. The vagaries of the international demand for these goods put the economies at the mercy of fluctuating world prices. Thus, many of the newly independent countries lack a solid financial underpinning. Current figures show they continue to depend on the export of raw materials. In Southeast Asia, Malaya is the least dependent—nevertheless, 80.1 per cent of her exports consist of raw materials. Other newly independent states show similar percentages: Burma, 97.2 per cent; Indonesia, 99 per cent; Sierra Leone, 85.7 per cent; Cameroon, 92 per cent; Angola, Kenya, Nigeria, Sudan, and Uganda, all over 98 per cent. To give the colonial powers their due, industrialization efforts were limited by low energy potentials: water power and liquid and hard fuels were scarce. In per capita energy potential, the developing nations average less than 5 per cent that of the United States.

Analysts of the problem of postindependence instability have argued that these factors are not as important as the means by which independence was attained. A number of elements present in the process of achieving independence have had their impact on the postindependence experiences of former colonies. If the nationalist movement is severely repressed, as it was in former French Indo-China, the nationalist leaders tend to grow more extreme and to refuse to cooperate with the colonial government. Because repression inhibits the interchange of ideas within the community, it can lead to future antagonisms.

Or, the road to independence may be violent, giving rise to the guerrilla-type war that is usually characteristic of wars for independence (as in Indonesia and Vietnam). Guerrilla warfare tends to be atomistic—small groups develop, exercising their own authority and deciding their own strategy. After independence, these divisions prove difficult to eliminate or to assimilate into peaceful civilian life. As the heritage of such warfare, large numbers of weapons remain available to dissident elements throughout the country. Violence becomes a way of life for many politicians and young men who are antagonistic to the slow give and take of civilian politics. Finally, the emotional anticolonialism wrought by long, bitter years of fighting endangers efforts to use foreign capital and expertise to rehabilitate these war-torn states. Examples of this antiforeign sentiment can be seen in Indonesia, Vietnam, and Algeria.

A third divisive element in the process of achieving independence is provided by certain unique institutional arrangements left by the colonial governments in the last days of their rule. For example, Dutch efforts to maintain control in Indonesia led to the establishment of artificial federal states, many of which were administered by anti-Republican leaders. Native reaction was expressed in the words of former Vice-President Mohammad Hatta: "A federal system is in fact suitable for such a far-flung archipelago and might be expected to strengthen the feeling of unity . . . [but] the manner and timing of the move by the Netherlands Indies Government had aroused such antipathy toward ideas of federation" that federalism was eliminated.[5] The French decided to grant independence to states, such as Upper Volta and Chad, whose capacity for survival as viable economic units was questionable, while the Belgians gave independence to the Congo —a country united in name only and ripe for the civil war that ensued.

In those countries—India, Malaysia, and the Philippines—which have achieved the most stable and, in each case, democratic political systems after at least five years of independence, what common elements exist? Certainly these countries do not appear to have inherited entirely beneficial situations. Each experienced civil strife in its early years: India, the conflict between Muslims and Hindus; the Philippines, the struggle with the Communist-led Huks; Malaysia, the ten-year guerrilla war against the Communists. Each suffered the impact of World War II—Malaysia and the Philippines were even occupied. All three are composed of diverse ethnic, language, and religious groups. The economies of all depend largely upon the export of primary products. All entered the period of independence with large-scale illiteracy (India's was over 80 per cent). These are the negative elements; what, if any, positive elements existed?

India, Malaysia, and the Philippines all experienced long periods of colonial rule. European control over parts of these countries was established as early as the sixteenth century. Because of the length of colonial domination, each developed a relatively better civil service— particularly at the senior levels—than her neighbors. In each case, the colonial language became the lingua franca of the elite, allowing them to communicate among themselves and to exchange ideas. Nationals of all three countries were allowed to seek higher education abroad and to establish institutions of higher learning within the country itself. Thus there was created an educated elite with experience in Western institutions and processes. Finally, in each case independence was achieved in a relatively peaceful manner. This does not mean that there were not long periods of struggle during which nationalist leaders were imprisoned and nationalist movements suppressed—but those who led the struggle for independence were pledged to peaceful processes and the ultimate achievement of constitutional government. In each case, independence resulted in the formation of relatively stable

[5] Mohammad Hatta, "Indonesia's Foreign Policy," *Foreign Affairs*, 31 (April, 1953), 441ff.

governments led by educated leaders, backed by trained civil servants, and maintaining close and friendly relations with their former colonial rulers. Nevertheless, those who would predict the future of former colonies should note that such a colonial heritage as that enjoyed by India, Malaysia, and the Philippines is very rare indeed.

SELECTED BIBLIOGRAPHY

Crocker, W., *Self-Government for the Colonies*. London: George Allen & Unwin, 1949.

Delavignette, R., *Freedom and Authority in French West Africa*. London: Oxford University Press, 1950.

Easton, S., *The Rise and Fall of Western Colonialism*. New York: Frederick A. Praeger, 1964.

———, *The Twilight of European Colonialism*. New York: Holt, Rinehart & Winston, Inc., 1960.

Emerson, R., *From Empire to Nation*. Cambridge, Mass.: Harvard University Press, 1960.

Furnivall, J., *Colonial Policy and Practice*. London: Cambridge University Press, 1948.

Ginsburg, N., *Atlas of Economic Development*. Chicago: University of Chicago Press, 1961.

Griffiths, Sir P., *The British Impact on India*. London: MacDonald & Co., Ltd., 1952.

Haines, G., *Africa Today*. Baltimore: Johns Hopkins Press, 1955.

Hodgkin, T., *Nationalism in Colonial Africa*. New York: New York University Press, 1957.

Moon, P. T., *Imperialism and World Politics*. New York: The Macmillan Company, 1927.

Panikkar, K., *Asia and Western Dominance*. London: George Allen & Unwin, 1953.

Perham, M., *The Colonial Reckoning*. New York: Alfred A. Knopf, Inc., 1962.

Plamenetz, J., *On Alien Rule and Self-Government*. New York: Longmans, Green & Co., Inc., 1960.

Pratt, J., *America's Colonial Experiment*. Englewood Cliffs, N. J.: Prentice-Hall, Inc., 1950.

van Mook, H., *The Stakes of Democracy in Southeast Asia*. New York: W. W. Norton & Company, Inc., 1950.

Wallerstein, I., *Social Change: The Colonial Situation*. New York: John Wiley & Sons, Inc., 1966.

III

THE SEARCH FOR NATIONAL IDENTITY

Prior to the entrance of Virginia into the War Between the States, Robert E. Lee is said to have agonized over his course of action in the approaching conflict: Was he first a citizen of Virginia or of the United States of America? This conflict between national loyalty and regional loyalty exists today in a variety of forms throughout the developing nations of the world. The difficulties in establishing national allegiance in such countries as the United Arab Republic, Nigeria, and Laos are obvious to the West, but the ramifications of the problem are often more subtle. Of considerable local importance are the ethnic, linguistic, tribal and religious divisions which do not attract the same degree of international attention. This political alienation, this lack of national identity or national loyalty, or—to oversimplify—this unwillingness or inability of an individual or a group to feel part of the state, shall be referred to as the problem of national identity or loyalty. This basic problem—that of developing a sense of national identity within pluralistic societies—will be analyzed on four levels: the types of disunity, their causes, their impact, and the nature of the efforts to eliminate them.

The lack of national identity in the developing areas manifests itself in a number of ways, but two of these have been of particular political importance in recent years. The first type, and that which has had the most violent repercussions, is found among those groups which have refused to submit to the authority of the central government. These ethnic, religious, and tribal groups insist on independence or —at the very least—autonomy. This schismatic development is, of course, not unknown in Europe or in the Western Hemisphere. It was one of the factors in the downfall of Austria-Hungary, the break-up of the ill-fated unions of Belgium and the Netherlands, of Spain and

Portugal, and of Norway and Sweden, and the constant turmoil in the Latin American republics. The most obvious twentieth-century parallels include the tribal and provincial disruptions in the Congo's post-independence years, the revolts by the Karens, the Shans, and other hill peoples in postwar Burma, the Ambonese insurrection against Indonesia which began with the end of Dutch rule, the revolts of the Kurds and the Armenians against various Middle Eastern governments, the efforts by the Nagas in eastern India to achieve autonomy, the Biafran war, and the Tibetan resistance to Communist China. In each case, the efforts of the central administration to impose its sovereignty resulted in civil war.

SECESSIONIST THREATS AND THEIR CAUSES

The general factors which give rise to a desire for complete autonomy or for special status will be considered, but several seem to be common to those cases already discussed. These elements may also be present in states which have not experienced internecine strife, but their presence among secessionist peoples is enlightening. Aside from the obvious differences present in most pluralistic societies, several potentially divisive factors exist.

1. RELIGION. With the possible exceptions of the secession of Katanga and the Kurdish rebellion, each of the conflicts mentioned arose, in part, because the faith of the controlling elements in the central government was different from that of the dissident group. The most articulate Karens are Christian in a Buddhist society; the Ambonese leadership is Christian in Muslim Indonesia; the Armenian Christians are "foreign" to the Middle East; the Nagas are animist and some of their leaders are Christian in Hindu-dominated India; Biafra has Christian leadership while the Nigerian Government is at least dominated by Moslems from the North. Buddhist Tibet differs sharply from professedly atheistic Communist China. It should be noted that although the dissident groups may include large numbers of members of the majority faith, the spokesmen for the group are usually members of the minority religion.

Religion supplies an emotional element with political and economic overtones. Particularly in areas (such as Burma and Indonesia) which were formerly under the domination of primarily Christian countries, those natives who accepted the religion of the colonial power received special privileges. Thus, when independence was achieved, the converts feared a loss of position and the nationalists remembered what they considered to be treacherous association with the colonial powers.

The friction which developed was even more regrettable because it resulted in the loss of many of the best-educated and best-trained people who either would not or could not work with the new leaders.

2. GEOGRAPHY. In each case, except Biafra, the greatest concentration of the disaffected is found outside the area of central administration and political development. In no case are large numbers of the minority group located close to majority groups. Most of the dissident groups are composed of hill peoples, or are located in areas where communications are poor, or—as in the case of Indonesia—are separated from the majority group by vast distances. These difficulties in communication have often been the chief causes of the conflict. Native scholars have usually done very little research on their own frontier areas; the best studies are often those made by Europeans during the colonial period. The ignorance in many of these countries of remote communities is sometimes appalling. This ignorance is not aided by Sunday-supplement articles or by government propaganda emphasizing the "brotherhood" and "close friendship" among the various peoples of the nation.

3. ADMINISTRATION. All the dissident groups mentioned above either enjoyed a semiautonomous status during the colonial period or were controlled by an administration other than that which controlled the rest of the state. The Belgians encouraged the separation of the Katangese in the Congo; the British gave special consideration to the Karens and to other hill tribes in Burma; the Ambonese in the former Dutch East Indies and the Kurds and Armenians in the Middle East had been treated separately for centuries; the Nagas had never been completely "civilized"; Biafra was directly ruled by the British, while the largest area of Nigeria was indirectly ruled, and the Ibos of Biafra dominated the colonial civil service; and Tibet had been an autonomous unit within the Chinese empire.

4. FOREIGN INVOLVEMENT. A comparatively common factor (though not universal) is the hope, often unrealized, of the dissident groups for foreign support in their efforts toward self-determination. This expectation may be naive, given the international situation, but it provides the stimulus for what have usually been abortive attempts to achieve independence. The Katangese expected and got support from Belgium and other foreign powers, but the Karens—who expected aid from the British, to whom they had long been loyal—received only private encouragement from members of Parliament and church leaders. The Dutch have been accused by the Indonesians of being responsible for the Ambonese revolt of 1950; the Armenians long considered it almost the duty of Christian nations to provide help; the Turkish Kurds were granted autonomy by the Allies after World War I. The Biafrans re-

ceived aid in the form of arms, food and mercenaries from abroad. Even the Nagas showed they were not completely primitive by appealing to the United Nations.

The few other cases of this type of estrangement also have these factors—in whole or in large part—in common. There remains one other variant which is not a cause but a result of this extreme variety of dissatisfaction: civil war. Civil strife has resulted in all of the cases discussed, but in none has the conclusion been entirely satisfactory to either side. Exhaustion of resources or the pressure of overwhelming odds may bring temporary respite in open conflict, but the basic disturbances continue.

PRESSURES FOR SPECIAL STATUS BY MINORITIES

A second manifestation of the problem of national identity is found among those who want, not complete independence or autonomy, but special constitutional guarantees of certain minority rights. The important word here is *constitutional,* although the constitutions in the states in question are often of a somewhat tenuous nature. The vital factor is that the guarantees must not be subject to future political negotiation; they are usually granted as a result of just such a process. Those seeking these guarantees are often groups which have been unsuccessful in gaining their primary goals through open warfare or who have never had the military power necessary to attempt secession. There is, therefore, at least grudging acceptance of the existing state.

In India, the result of this negotiation has been the establishment of states along linguistic lines (against the better judgment of sections of the Congress Party leadership). Since the establishment of Andhra in 1953, the majority of India's fourteen states have been reorganized along these lines. In Lebanon, the constitution assures that "the sects shall be equally represented in public employment and in the Cabinet," and reserves the presidency to the Maronite Christians, the premiership to Sunnite Muslims, and the position of Speaker of the House to the Shi'ite Muslims. In the Malaysian constitution, the paramount ruler (Yang di-Pertuan Agong) is called upon to protect the "special position of the Malays, and the legitimate interests of other communities," and the governmental system is carefully designed to safeguard the Malays from Chinese incursions. Negotiations for the abortive federation with Singapore displayed even more careful constitutional guarantees to Malays in the face of Singapore's large Chinese population. The constitution of Cyprus, like that of Lebanon, contains special provisions under which Greeks and Turks are guaranteed parliamentary representation and particular state offices.

These arrangements may appear tenuous and at times the minority groups do resort to paramilitary operations (as in Lebanon in 1958), but the system has such important reasons for continuance that the status quo ante is usually restored. This is in spite of the fact that in most instances the causal variables are similar to the factors responsible for the first type—i.e., ethnic, religious, and administrative differences. However, at least in the cases discussed, there are variations from the first extreme which may account for the more moderate approach. Perhaps most important, in such cases the minority is usually not geographically separated from the majority; instead, the two are intermingled within a comparatively small area. Administratively, this makes division more difficult; psychologically, it lessens the feeling of alienation. Furthermore, it has become apparent to the leadership, at times through the hard lesson of civil war, that it is less cataclysmic to live together peacefully than to fight continually. It should be noted that constitutional guarantees are often the price paid for such a peace. In some cases, as in Cyprus, outside pressure has been used to gain the necessary accommodation. Foreign influence is particularly vital when a colony will not be granted independence unless constitutional guarantees to minorities are provided. Of course, agreements made under foreign pressure often do not last beyond the early years of independence.

Finally, there are efforts to achieve special consideration through political bargaining among groups who accept the new state and pledge loyalty to it. In this third manifestation of the problem of national identity, there is no estrangement from the established state and normally there is no effort to obtain guarantees of sectional rights in the constitution. Thus, there is no alienation as such. If no one ethnic, religious, or language group is dominant, others may not feel the necessity for constitutional protection; and if party structures cross group lines to include a variety of political and social interests, political accommodation may appear more feasible. This sort of political bargaining is to be found among ethnic groups in the Philippines, Indonesia, and Tanzania.

GENERAL OBSTACLES TO NATIONAL UNITY

The causal factors responsible for particular types of political alienation have been discussed. Now more general causal variables, related to a lack of national loyalty, will be considered. Any one state's development may be a unique combination of these or other elements:

1. The establishment of "artificial" states.
2. The establishment of artificial borders.
3. Colonial policies.
4. Village and regional parochialism.
5. Improperly socialized minorities.

1. "ARTIFICIAL" STATES. Essential to an understanding of the problem of "artificial" states is acknowledgment of the fact that most of the states of the Afro-Asian world and all of the Latin American nations did not exist as national entities prior to their colonization by European powers. Indeed, the concept of the nation was foreign to many of these communities. Sometimes based upon a conglomeration of different tribal groups, often centered upon old kingdoms, and almost always confined by boundaries determined by imperial ambitions rather than ethnic, linguistic, or political considerations, these colonies were called upon to become new nations almost overnight. It was to be expected that some groups would not become properly nationalized.

First, almost all the new nations in Africa and several in Asia were under the control of colonial powers for a comparatively short period of time. Administration of the interior of sub-Sahara Africa began only at the end of the nineteenth century and ended, in most cases, by 1960. Intense influence by one administration binding diverse peoples endured only for a matter of decades. Even in Indonesia—which was ruled for some three hundred years by the Dutch—dissident groups were not totally pacified until the twentieth century. Thus, the time necessary to establish a sense of national identity was not available.

A second problem resulted from the combining of diverse peoples within one administrative area. Given the short period of colonial domination, this local patriotism or friction could not be erased. Thus, in Uganda, independence was delayed by the nationalism of the once proudly independent nation of Buganda, which became a protectorate only in 1894 and was never completely incorporated into the colony of Uganda. Nigeria was united during World War I; only a few years prior to independence, one of the country's foremost politicians, Oba-femi Awolowo, remarked: "Nigeria is not a nation. It is a mere political expression." Independence thus found strong regional feelings in East, West, and North Nigeria ultimately leading to civil war.

A final ramification of disunity rising out of the "artificiality" of the nation has been the lateness of nationalist developments, a factor obviously tied to the first two points. National rather than regional organization, leadership, and ideology have been late in arriving in most Afro-Asian states and even in Latin America. The Europeanized nationalists usually found it difficult to form ties with the more traditional rural community. Thus, the population has not had the internal leadership necessary to build a sense of national identity. This delay can be seen in former British colonies in Africa, where nationalism developed only after World War II; in Southeast Asia, where Indonesian political leaders spoke of "Javanese" nationalism until the 1920's, Malayan nationalism was a postwar phenomenon, and Burmese nationalist movements were limited to the Buddhist majority until just before independence. This "artificiality" was often hidden by the tight control of colonial administrations, which kept down intergroup outbreaks and gave protection and a feeling of security to ethnic and other minorities. However, when independence removed these controls and safeguards, the divisions became all too apparent.

2. ARTIFICIAL BORDERS. A closely related problem is illustrated by Ghana's Prime Minister, Kwame Nkrumah, who states in his autobiography that he was born on the border of what was then the Gold Coast to a tribe divided by French and British colonial administrations. This and other borders established in the nineteenth and early twentieth centuries in Africa and Asia were responsible for a lack of national unity and loyalty in a number of countries. Because tribal, ethnic, and linguistic groups were divided by colonial boundaries and because the fractured minorities were not sufficiently socialized into the colony, the individual's loyalty often remained with a regional group which cut across the new boundaries. Thus, many Shans living in Burma, China, and Thailand have only tenuous national loyalties. Similar situations have developed in West Africa, where boundary lines run inland from the coast, cutting across the traditional ethnic, tribal, and religious bonds that run parallel to the coast. The complexity of this situation was further increased after World War I when two former German colonies—the Cameroons and Togoland—were divided into British and French mandates, thus redividing tribes.

Additional difficulties arising from the boundaries drawn by the imperial powers result from the fact that the continent of Africa hosts a number of small colonies with little ethnic, economic, or military reason for existence. As one writer on Africa remarked:

Most of the present colonial boundaries were fixed in the nineteenth century, mainly for political reasons and under very different conditions from those which obtain today. The result has been that some colonies are too small for their governments ever to be able to provide efficiently or economically the large variety of services needed in the modern African state.[1]

Added to these administrative problems are the indistinct ethnic or geographic divisions which exist among many colonies. An excellent example of this is Gambia, which one writer describes as an anomaly which "defies all principles of boundary-making. There are no geographical features or other lines of demarcation, whether economic, cultural, or racial, separating it from the country surrounding it." [2] Similar statements can be made regarding Portuguese Guinea, Rio De Oro, and French Somaliland. Given the minuteness of the tribal entity, these enclaves have until recently presented few international political problems. Having little relative economic importance in themselves, they are the vestiges of former trading posts or the fruits of diplomatic barter. This peaceful situation may not last, given the history of nationalism elsewhere and the desire to incorporate the last traces of colonialism into larger, independent entities.

These last areas of colonialism can also lead to international disunity and strife as their neighbors clash over the spoils. Thus, Somalia and Kenya argue over areas in northern Kenya; Malaysia, Indonesia, and the Philippines have threatened one another over the colonial territories of Borneo that have been incorporated into Malaysia; and the Portuguese territories in Africa appear ripe for conflict. Irredentist claims are not looked upon with favor by the more responsible Afro-Asian leaders, who fear the Pandora's box of conflicts that might be opened by countries with artificial borders, divided tribes, and pre-colonial claims to territory. Even if they do not lead to war, these frictions can cause serious internal disruptions as states neglect domestic improvements in order to increase their military budgets (see Malaysia's budget following Indonesia's confrontation policy).

3. COLONIAL POLICY. Much has been written and proclaimed about the supposed colonial policy of "divide and rule" and such a policy obviously would be a major force for disunity. In spite of nationalist exhortations to the contrary, colonial policy was not so precisely defined. However, the current emphasis is on those particular factors in colonial rule which kept populations divided, not on the often

---

[1] T. R. Batten, *Problems of African Development* (London: Oxford University Press, 1948), Part II, 157-58.
[2] E. W. Evans, *Britannia Overseas* (London: Thomas Nelson & Sons, 1946), pp. 55-56.

extensive efforts by colonial powers to unite diverse peoples by establishing communication networks, stable administration, and appropriate ethnic and social policies.

Two types of administrative systems, however, maintained former divisions or provided the basis for future national disunity. The methods of colonial administration followed by the Belgians and postnineteenth century Portuguese, although differing markedly in the areas of education and economic and social development, are examples of the efficient dimming of national consciousness and the creation of fragmented states. Three major elements of these policies were and are factors which diminish the possibility of a sense of national identity. First, in neither colonial system were efforts made to build national parties or to bring together political leaders from various regions. In the areas under Portuguese control, nationalist parties are forbidden and the highly limited colonial administrations are composed almost entirely of Portuguese and of an extremely small group of *assimilados* (those natives "civilized" enough to be considered equal to Europeans). The very thought of an independent Angola or Mozambique is denied by the concept of a single Portuguese state, combining the motherland and overseas territories.

The Belgian Congo did not have true national parties before independence (and even now the term *national* is questionable); as late as 1951, only eight of the thirty-three members of the central legislative council were Africans. This gave no chance for African politicians to meet together, to discuss common problems, or to come to know one another. The events in the Congo after independence are the results of these policies. A second factor was the Belgians' decision not to educate Africans for higher positions until the 1950s, thus making impossible the creation of a group of men trained in statecraft and perpetuating parochial or regional attitudes in political life. Finally, very few natives were trained in the language of the colonial power or in any universal indigenous tongue. This destroyed—or, more accurately, never prepared—the way for communication, particularly on the lower level, thereby diminishing opportunities to establish national discussions, symbols, and myths.

Still another colonial policy which was later to cause disunity was the method of indirect rule inaugurated by the British and the Dutch, under which territories were controlled through indigenous rulers and administrators rather than directly through the appointed civil servants. For example, the administrative structure in parts of the Dutch East Indies was as follows:

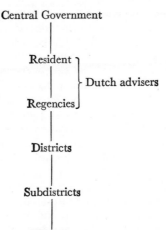

Actual control was often in the hands of British or Dutch "advisers," who saw to it that the administration of the area adhered to general colonial policy. In practice, the limits of power of the native authorities varied—even within the same colony. Where most successful, the façade of indigenous rule, with all its ceremonial accouterments, was carefully maintained.

Indirect rule was considered desirable for three reasons: it decreased the number of Europeans necessary to control the outlying regions; it brought loyalty and peace to the colony by maintaining old traditions (and some argued that there was intrinsic merit in traditional society as such); and it dampened feelings of nationalism by directing both loyalty and criticism toward the local ruler rather than toward the colonial administration. Indirect rule was particularly effective in discouraging nationalism and unity when it was applied only to part of a country, as was the case in the former Dutch East Indies, Nigeria, and Burma. Although direct rule hastened nationalism by directing dissatisfaction to the central government, the areas under indirect rule—usually the outlying regions—were less than eager for independence, for the people had no national consciousness and the rulers feared the loss of their positions. Thus, Northern Nigeria, the hill tribes of Burma, and the outlying islands of the Indonesian archipelago were all less fervently nationalist than other parts of the colonies, while some sections of the population in these areas were openly procolonial. As one Karen leader put it: "The

Karens owe what progress and advancement they have made to the missionaries whom they affectionately call their 'Mother' under the British government whom they rightly call 'Father.' " [3]

Support for the colonial administration was particularly strong among converts to Christianity and other minority groups who were depended upon by the government to provide civil servants and military personnel. Minorities were considered less likely to bring their military training to bear against the government for the nationalist cause, and Christians were expected to be missionary-trained to Western ways. The result of all this was the buttressing of local loyalties by maintaining traditional rulers, providing arms and military training for defense, and giving status in the colonial society—all of which led to serious defections from the national state after independence.

4. VILLAGE AND REGIONAL PAROCHIALISM. It should be noted that the developing areas are well behind the West in the transportation of goods and the communication of ideas. Road and rail densities in Africa, Latin America, and Southeast Asia (with minor exceptions, such as the Indian subcontinent) are well below the world mean. [4] Practically every independent state in sub-Sahara Africa and Southeast Asia has a newspaper circulation of less than 20 per 1000 inhabitants (the United States rate is 325; that of the United Kingdom —the highest—is 570). Although these former colonial areas have not been static, their numbers of radios, television sets, and other means of mass communication of ideas remain low. Even the money economy may not yet have affected large sections of the population; added to other problems, such as linguistic and religious diversity, it may even serve to intensify parochial loyalties and antagonisms. The result is that rural inhabitants look to local political, social, and religious leaders. Myths, symbols, and heroes are local or regional, rather than national. Perhaps only one or two men in a village may be able to identify national parties and leaders, while the rest of the inhabitants remain centered around village problems. Attitudes toward other parts of the nation—where they exist at all—may be more nearly described as suspicious than as antagonistic. The elimination of this parochialism is one of the chief aims of nationalist politicians, who see its continuance in the perpetuation of regional rather than national loyalties and traditional rather than modern attitudes toward change.

It is interesting to note that many new states have made efforts to

[3] San C. Po, *Burma and the Karens* (London: Sidney Kiek & Son, Ltd., 1929), p. 58.
[4] See N. Ginsburg, *Atlas of Economic Development* (Chicago: University of Chicago Press, 1961) for information.

provide each village with a radio so that national news, culture, and doctrine can be disseminated. The best example of a nation in which poor communications have been partially responsible for a serious lack of national identity is Laos. Without railroads or good radio transmission, with one of the poorest road density ratings in the world (and few of the roads are passable during the long monsoon season), and with the fifth lowest newspaper circulation per capita, national unity is not great.

5. UNSOCIALIZED MINORITIES. All these factors contribute to the existence of unsocialized minorities—groups which have not accepted the loyalty patterns of the majority. This is true, not only of the new states of Africa and Asia, but also of the older states in Latin America. For instance, in Peru about one third of the population remains outside national life, not interested in or appealed to by the central government. In the Afro-Asian world, the existence of these unsocialized minorities has led to serious political frictions and even to military conflicts. It is not a problem which has been alleviated with independence—indeed, the opposite may be true, for independence has caused traditional divisions to grow wider in Ceylon, Burma, Laos, Nigeria, and the Congo.

EXPRESSIONS OF ALIENATION

Thus, a variety of forces has left many countries with groups which have no loyalty or attachment to the state or which desire only to preserve their special identity within it. The methods used to express their alienation from the controlling society or the separate character of their particular group are also varied. These reactions may be considered under three headings: social divisions, paramilitary operations, and constitutional or political accommodation.

1. PERPETRATION OF CULTURAL DIFFERENCES. Unique clothing, customs, and religion have long been means of emphasizing the identity of a group in an alien society. When strenuous efforts are being made to nationalize a community, the reaction of these groups is often to strengthen such distinctions. For example, during the troubles between the Shans and the Burmans, one Shan prince is said to have threatened his son-in-law with banishment if he continued to wear Burman dress. Some Malayan nationalists have decried the wearing of the Indian dhoti by politicians. Such examples abound, but although they provide the foundation for disunity, they are not intrinsically dangerous to the security of the state.

Of somewhat greater seriousness are the efforts of minority groups to preserve their own schools, language, and religion. Differences in religion do not necessarily lead to conflict unless, as in Burma, the majority group attempts to establish a religious state, or, as among the Muslims of West Africa, religion forms the basis for international sectarian attachments. The matter of education and language can have long-range consequences for the unity of the state, however, particularly when minority or foreign-language groups are allowed to establish their own schools (as in the case of the Chinese in Southeast Asia). This problem may be somewhat alleviated by the teaching of the national language in the secondary schools and in universities, but poorly trained language teachers and the fact that many students do not go on to such schools diminish the effectiveness of this program. The result is that minority demands for separate schools result in the continuance—and, at times, the reinforcement—of sectionalism and parochialism, thus further alienating the community from the majority. A particular problem, evident in areas attempting to establish a national language, is the conflict between those (usually the better educated) who are fluent in the colonial tongue and those who desire to "nationalize" the native language. This may cause the alienation of the best-trained and most highly educated individuals within the society. The language issue may also alienate long-term foreign residents and those of mixed blood, who often place greater importance on things Western than even the Europeans do.

Even social statistics have their place in these controversies. The most notable example is Lebanon, where a national census has not been taken since 1932 so as not to upset the delicate population balance between Muslim and Christian. A new census, showing a heavy increase in one of the two groups, might well lead to civil war. Other states, India and China among them, have been known to attempt to alleviate the minority problem by rearranging census data so as to "eliminate" minority groups. In India, the 1941 census lists 25 million tribal members, while that of 1951 lists only 1.7 million. Not all tribes were incorporated into other groups, nor is the difference to be accounted for by the creation of Pakistan. Nor can the manipulation of statistics so easily eradicate the factors which form the basis for continued political friction and estrangement.

2. PARAMILITARY REVOLT. A far more serious expression of discontent with the majority is paramilitary activity. This reaction is normally to be found among those who do not accept the authority of the state and who continue to strive for independence. Even those who desire only special consideration within the new state may resort to violent means to attain their ends. In the twentieth century, ethnic

and religious groups that have taken up arms against the central government include the Moros of the Philippines, the Darul Islam and various ethnic groups of the outer islands in Indonesia, the tribesmen of Laos, the hill peoples of Thailand, the Kachins, Karens, Shans, Mons, and Arakanese in Burma, the Nagas in India, the frontier tribesmen in Pakistan and China, the Kurds and Armenians in the Middle East, various tribal groups in the Congo, the Ibos in Nigeria, and the Greeks and Turks in Cyprus. These conflicts have ranged from small skirmishes to full-scale civil war.

An extreme case occurred with the Burmese government's efforts to gain the loyalty—or, at least, the cooperation—of its minorities. Almost immediately after Burma won its independence in 1948, the Christian-led Karens began military operations in an effort to win their own independence from the new state. "Trotskyist" and "Stalinist" Communists had revolted earlier. By 1949, other insurgent political-military units had developed. The harassed government, whose power was at one point confined to the area within a five-mile radius of the capital, Rangoon, succeeded in breaking this iron grip. But it continued to be faced with isolated rebellions: the efforts of escaping Nationalist Chinese troops (KMT) to establish a state within a state, and armed revolts by the Shans, Kachins, Mons, and Muslims. The Karens, Kachins, Mons, and Shans wanted either independence or almost complete regional autonomy. Unable to get this peacefully, in spite of a constitution which gave some groups the right to secede, these minorities entered into open warfare with the government. In 1960, more than ten years after the stranglehold on Rangoon had been broken, Burma's first military government (1958–60) proudly announced that rebels in the field included only:

White Flag Communists	700
Red Flag Communists	209
KNDO (Karens)	1695
Shans	274
KMT	2317
Mujahids	290[5]

[5] *Union of Burma, Is Trust Vindicated?* (Rangoon: Government Printing Office, 1960), p. 35.

It is not entirely clear how it was possible to make so exact a count in the field. Two years later, after a civilian interregnum, it was reported that there were 3–4000 Karen rebels, 2–3000 Shan insurgents, 1500 White Flag Communists, and 500 Red Flag Communists in the field. But, the government promised, it would soon be possible to drive safely between the two main cities of Mandalay and Rangoon. When a second military coup gave the army control of the government in March, 1962, it was announced that the "federal problem" was the major reason for its seizure of power—but as of 1969 Burma was still struggling with dissident ethnic, religious, and ideological rebels.

Few states have experienced difficulties as acute and enduring as those of Burma, but paramilitary reactions have not been unusual in the developing nations. They can be most effective where the insurgents are based in less accessible areas, when they get supplies from and find hiding places in local villages, and where arms are easily obtainable from defectors and smugglers or left over from earlier wars. All these elements are present in Burma and, in fact, throughout Southeast Asia. The problem is made more difficult by the fact that, unlike the American and Spanish civil wars, these operations may be pursued on a very minor scale: the "soldier" is usually a peasant who takes part in military operations on something of an ad hoc basis. Thus, these conflagrations, if such they can be called, may endure for a number of years.

3. DEMANDS FOR CONSTITUTIONAL GUARANTEES OF MINORITY RIGHTS. Certain efforts of minority groups to gain constitutional guarantees of particular rights have been discussed. These provisions have taken the form of the creation of states along linguistic lines, the official acceptance of minority languages, the guarantee of representation in national and regional assemblies, the reservation of particular offices to members of minority groups or the establishment of a system under which such offices are rotated among members of different groups, the formation of an upper legislative chamber in which the minority is overrepresented, the passage of sumptuary laws, and so on. On the one hand, these provisions are the price paid to keep the minorities in the national fold; on the other, acceptance of these guarantees by the dissident group usually implies agreement to operate within the state although not necessarily identification with it.

A second type of political effort which may be made by discontented groups is that directed toward the establishment of a system of federalism, hopefully with a provision for later secession. The idea of federalism has not been greatly favored by the nationalist leaders of the developing nations. It is considered divisive and detrimental to national unity. Where it has been granted, it has taken a highly limited form. Among all the new states of Africa, only Nigeria had a working federal system (until it was eliminated by the military). In Asia, Malaysia has a federal constitution and India has been termed a quasifederal state. In Indonesia, the very word *federalism* suggests a Dutch plot; if a federal system is ever formed there, it must go under another name.

An analysis of the possible reactions of dissident groups should take into account the fact that the existence of one reaction in a state does not preclude the existence of others; in fact, it is probably indicative of their presence.

POLICIES TO STRENGTHEN NATIONAL UNITY

Political life in the developing areas is not static, and natural changes, as well as formal policies, are helping to alleviate the general problem discussed in this chapter. Parochialism and regional loyalties are disintegrating while nationalist politicians have been developing plans for the unification of their countries. The greater mobility of populations has had a particular impact on localism; villagers have been able to travel to other places and have seen the influences of the outside world infiltrate their previously isolated communities. On the other hand, G. W. Skinner, in *Local, Ethnic, and National Loyalties in Village Indonesia,* points out that such mobility may not automatically widen loyalties but may instead encourage closer attachment to traditional attitudes:

> Ethnic awareness is intensified by interethnic contact, and ethnic loyalties come to the fore only when the members of the group recognize common interests vis-à-vis others. It is notably those ethnic groups whose members during the last half-century of Dutch rule were most mobile and most avidly in pursuit of scarce ends in the larger society which are outstanding today for ethnic loyalties bordering on chauvinism.[6]

The villager, then, is less aware of his ethnic loyalties until he comes in contact with other communities—but he is also unaware of the nation as a whole. Local patriotism may become greater after such contact, but an individual can never develop a sense of national identity if (as is true of many in Laos) he does not know what country he lives in! This contact—and, perhaps, the competition between loyalties to which it leads—is a necessary prelude to a wider nationalism.

Mobility of populations increased during the colonial period. Peace, the disintegration of old boundaries, the extension of roads, and the

---

[6] *Local, Ethnic, and National Loyalties in Village Indonesia* (New Haven, Conn.: Yale University Cultural Report Series, No. 8, 1959), p. 7.

introduction of other forms of communication were all factors in this increase. Another policy of the colonial administrations which sent people from their villages was the introduction of Western health standards. By lowering the death rate and extending the lifespan, the European powers helped to increase the pressure on the land and to force people into the cities. World War II multiplied contacts with the outside world as military bases were established by the Allies, remote areas were occupied by the Japanese or Germans, and young men from the colonies went off to war in faraway places. (In Ghana, for example, an important event in nationalist history was the riot staged by returned servicemen.)

This mobility has increased still further in the postindependence period. At times, this mobility has been caused by special circumstances: the forced movement of populations after the partition of India, the widescale insurgency in the Congo, Burma, and Malaysia which forced rural populations to seek security in the cities; or, the bitter fruits of defeat, one of which is the Arab refugee problem. Other movements have been more natural: individuals have sought greater opportunities in the independent states, and postwar air travel has opened up hitherto inaccessible areas. Thus, over time, national awareness would have developed naturally, but this process has been accelerated by the considerable efforts of the new nationalist governments.

1. NATIONAL POLITICS. Political activities are encouraged to further specific goals but also from a sincere desire to establish a unified state. In the first instance, this process provides an excellent rationale for the urbanized nationalist elites to diminish the powers of local chiefs, headmen, and princes who did not fully cooperate with the nationalist movement. This policy of weakening regional power can best be seen in Ghana, where Nkrumah engaged in strenuous efforts to "destool" recalcitrant chiefs. A second aid to unity, which also furthers political ambitions, is the extension of political parties to outlying regions. National parties thus not only bring new ideas and symbols to these areas but also become multi-ethnic, thereby diminishing the fragmentation of society. Other policies adopted after independence have also helped to develop a stronger feeling of national identity.

The first national elections bring the state to the entire country, as it were. As Skinner remarks with regard to the 1955 elections in Indonesia: "The election campaigns brought the Indonesian state into the immediate awareness of the villagers and in general fostered national loyalties of all kinds." [7] But elections and parties may be

[7] *Local, Ethnic, and National Loyalties,* p. 9.

divisive as well, splitting formerly united villages and ethnic groups along new lines or sharpening old differences. However, this sort of competition is, in some ways, necessary if local parochialism is to be replaced with an awareness of national goals. Local parties and their symbols may appeal to narrow ethnic or religious loyalties, as they often do in India; nevertheless, these organizations are attempting to gain representation in a national parliament, where they will make national policy. When a single party is dominant, as is the case in most new states, the nationalizing effect of elections and politics is even more obvious.[8]

2. PATRIOTISM AND PROPAGANDA. New leaders may inaugurate national symbols and myths. Of course, each state quickly begins to collect the paraphernalia of statehood, such as a flag, an anthem, postage stamps, coinage, and so forth, which may or may not have much impact on outlying areas. A number of countries have a "national day," at which time peoples from throughout the land are brought together both to symbolize unity and to foster it. Government funds have been used to distribute the national dress to minority groups. The names of streets, towns, and islands have been changed to eliminate memories of colonialism and to recall national heroes and history. Military service is used to instill nationalism and to socialize rural and regional peoples. After completing their military service, these men return to their villages to indoctrinate their fellow villagers.

Modern "history" is often reworked in order to build up the national leader and his party, to denigrate the colonial period, and to give to the nation greater importance on the world scene than it actually enjoys. Many of these states, composed as they were of diverse groups, were without a common history. It often became necessary to extend the history of the majority group or to invent a common background for the different groups. Early history and legends are usually vague enough to allow for this sort of "reinterpretation." As Thomas Hodgkin has so intriguingly put it:

If the apologists for European rule present this Hobbesian picture of a pre-European Africa in which there was "no account of Time; no Arts; no Letters; no Society; and, which is worst of all, continuall feare, and danger of violent death; And the life of man, solitary, poore, nasty, brutish, and short"—it is natural that the advocates of African self-government should reply with a Rousseauian picture of an African Golden Age of

[8] See A. Zolberg, "Mass Parties and National Integration: The Case of the Ivory Coast," *Journal of Politics*, 25 (1963), for an interesting view of this point.

perfect liberty, equality, and fraternity. The Hobbesian myth, taken literally, is nonsense. But the nationalist countermyth involves the same tendency to hypostatise "the African past," when there are in fact many diverse
African pasts. What is important, however, is that this process of rewriting
preconceptions is taking place on an increasing scale.[9]

3. NATIONAL LANGUAGES AND EDUCATION. Most vital to unity are
national languages and systems of education. The usefulness of education in the nationalizing process is obvious. It should be noted, however, that where most of the population is more than 80 per cent illit-
erate, as in most of tropical Africa, nationalization through education
is not a simple undertaking. The problem of language also presents obstacles. The nationalists agree that the preservation of a multitude of languages, with no common language to serve as a means of
communication, is not desirable—but agreement often stops there.
Should the language of the former colonial power be kept, since it is
known by the elite and is a means of contact with the outside world?
Should an indigenous language be used—and, if there is more than
one, which?

No single solution has been found. Obviously, the problem is most
acute in countries with no common indigenous tongue, such as most
of the new states in sub-Sahara Africa and a number of countries in
Asia. The difficulties of the situation can best be seen by briefly review-
ing the policies of three "adolescent" states: the Philippines, Indonesia,
and India.

The Philippines finds itself with approximately seventy native languages, plus two borrowed ones (Spanish and English) which were
the official languages during most of the twentieth century and, in
spite of a certain deterioration, are the most useful as common tongues.
But nationalism called for a native lingua franca. In 1946, Tagalog,
the native speech of 19 per cent of the population, was chosen. Although "Movie Tagalog" has become popular, efforts to establish a
high-quality literary language for the entire nation have not been
successful. Much more fruitful has been the inauguration of Behasa
Indonesia in a land with no common tongue except the now suspect
Dutch. Originally pushed by Indonesian nationalists (one of whom
demonstrated that Greek classics could be translated into Indonesian),
the language has its roots in "market Malay" which was a sort of
pigeon English spoken in market towns. Indonesian has become highly
eclectic, absorbing Arabic religious words and English and Dutch

[9] *Nationalism in Colonial Africa* (New York: New York University Press, 1957),
pp. 174-75.

scientific terms. A national institute has been created to fill the gaps in what was once a very primitive means of economic intercourse. Through strenuous national efforts, this artificial language has become the lingua franca of the country, although local languages remain strong. India, however, has gone in the opposite direction, in spite of her desire to make Hindi the national language. The existence of the lingual states is really an admission of defeat and a confirmation of separateness. What the outcome will be in the new African states is not predictable at present.

4. ANTIGUERRILLA MEASURES. Guerrilla warfare may help unite the country. The most successful antiguerrilla programs have incorporated social and economic development measures designed to win the support of the people. These measures include the education and/or indoctrination of populations, an emphasis on the development of better means of communications, an increase in the proportion of young men entering military service, and a heightened emphasis on nationalism. For example, in the not always successful antiguerrilla activities in South Vietnam, the government established *agrovilles,* in which rural populations were brought together for protection, education, and social and economic development. Later, it created strategic hamlets which were designed primarily for defense but which also provided educational and social services. Although it perhaps did not endear the regime to all, this process did create and encourage some common elements in the rural population.

SELECTED BIBLIOGRAPHY

Anderson, C., F. von der Mehden, and C. Young, *Issues of Political Development.* Englewood Cliffs, N. J.: Prentice-Hall, Inc., 1967.

Coleman, J., *Nigeria: Background to Nationalism.* Berkeley: University of California Press, 1958.

Deutsch, K. and W. Foltz, *Nation-Building.* New York: Atherton Press, 1963.

Emerson, R., *From Empire to Nation.* Cambridge, Mass.: Harvard University Press, 1960.

Feith, H., *Decline of Constitutional Democracy in Indonesia.* Ithaca, N. Y.: Cornell University Press, 1962.

Geertz, C., *Old Societies and New States.* New York: The Free Press, 1963.

Harrison, S., *The Most Dangerous Decades.* New York: Columbia University Press, 1957.

Lemarchand, R., "The Limits of Self-Determination: Katanga," *American Political Science Review,* 54 (June, 1960), 404–16.

Lerner, D., *The Passing of Traditional Society.* New York: Free Press of Glencoe, Inc., 1958.

Pye, L., *Communication and Political Development.* Princeton, N. J.: Princeton University Press, 1963.

Shibutani, T. and K. Kwan, *Ethnic Stratification: A Comparative Approach.* New York: The Macmillan Company, 1965.

Skinner, G. W. (ed.), *Local, Ethnic, and National Loyalties in Village Indonesia.* New Haven, Conn.: Yale University Cultural Report Series, No. 8, 1959.

Smith, W. Cantwell, *Islam in Modern History.* Princeton, N. J.: Princeton University Press, 1951.

von der Mehden, F. R., *Religion and Nationalism in Southeast Asia.* Madison: University of Wisconsin Press, 1963.

Wallerstein, I., "Ethnicity and National Integration in West Africa," *Cahiers d'études africaines,* 3 (1960), 129–39.

Wriggens, W., *Ceylon: Dilemmas of a New Nation.* Princeton, N. J.: Princeton University Press, 1960.

IV

Political Parties in the Developing Nations

The political party, in various forms, has been one element of the Western heritage which has been accepted in almost all the developing nations. Often, the "party" is only a short-lived parliamentary faction without local organization; at times, it is established by governmental decree. In some cases, its only role is to inform the nonparty rulers of popular dissatisfaction which may have developed, although in others it performs the same functions as it does in Western Europe and the United States. However, with few exceptions, every new state has accepted the formal structure of party government—if not its Western organization, processes, and goals. An analysis of the different types of party systems established in the developing nations must also consider the reasons for their existence, the question of interparty competition, and the impact of party systems on national unity.

Any classification of political parties in the approximately one hundred countries under consideration presents three immediate problems which cannot be solved to anyone's complete satisfaction. First, there is the element of time. The categories presented are based on the political situation as of early 1969; given the ephemeral nature of many organizations in developing countries, changes may be expected. The general pattern, however, has maintained itself for a number of years.

The next problem is one of definition; more precisely: How is *party* to be defined? The definition used here is intentionally broad, in order that it may encompass the variety of organizations which describe themselves as "parties." Therefore, a party will be defined as an organized group which seeks the control of the personnel and policies of government—a group that pays at least lip service to a principle or a set of principles, including the electoral process. The elections may not be fair, nor may there be a meaningful choice offered at the polls. In the elections of a majority of the states listed here, the final outcome has been well-known beforehand but the formalities of the democratic electoral process continue. In many cases it is this symbolic support which distinguishes *party* from *military junta*.

Finally, the classifications used here are, probably necessarily, somewhat arbitrary. Six categories have been employed, each based upon the number of parties effectively operating in the state. Within each, several variables have also been noted. Of particular interest in each case has been the element of competition within the party system.

NONCOMPETITIVE SYSTEMS

1. STATES THAT HAVE NO PARTIES OR IN WHICH PARTIES DO NOT PLAY EFFECTIVE GOVERNMENTAL ROLES (37 STATES).

Afghanistan	Ghana	Nigeria[1]	Yemen
Algeria	Haiti	Panama[1]	
Argentina[1]	Indonesia[1]	Paraguay	
Bahrein	Iraq	Peru[1]	
Bhutan	Jordan	Saudi Arabia	
Brazil[1]	Kuwait	Sierra Leone[1]	
Burma	Laos	Syria	
Burundi	Libya	Thailand	
Congo (Kin.)	Mali	Togo	
Dahomey	Morocco	United Arab Republic	
Ecuador[1]	Muscat Oman	Upper Volta	
Ethiopia	Nepal	Western Samoa	

[1] Recent military coup leaves situation fluid.

Two major differences are to be found within these thirty-seven states. Twelve countries (such as Ethiopia, Libya, and Saudi Arabia) have not yet found it necessary or desirable to accept the existence of political parties. Still governed by traditionalist rulers, most of these states are without legal organized opposition, and—with rare exceptions such as Western Samoa—their rulers do not uphold the principle of popular participation in government. The others have had one form or another of party rule in the past, but—largely because of military coups (as in Burma, Nigeria, Iraq, Ghana, and Mali) or strongman rule (as in Haiti and Paraguay)—parties actually play no effective role in determining the policies of government. In increasingly fewer cases the façade of a party system has been maintained and the promoters of military coups are remaining for longer periods. But almost all decisions continue to be made by the ruling hierarchies—several of which promise that democracy and true party competition will be permitted at some indefinite future date, but assert that the situation is not at present "ripe" for such developments. There have been efforts in the UAR and Burma to establish government-controlled parties, but these attempts have not been noted for their success. The life of legal parties under such conditions remains tenuous; and well-organized parties with local units are not looked upon with favor by the rulers of these countries. A proposition, not presently provable, is that the acceptance of the symbols attached to a party provides the basis for later popular participation in government.

The role of the party in influencing national unity and establishing loyalty to the state is recognized even among those regimes which allow political parties no effective role in making decisions. For example, the Revolutionary Councils of the United Arab Republic and Burma have made efforts to form government-controlled political organizations. In each case, the party was to act as the vanguard of the revolution and to muster public support of the programs of the military government. Neither government has been completely successful in these ventures, either because of opposition from political leaders or because of its own inability to control the party once it was formed. Authoritarian governments may also view political parties as a necessary safety valve through which the pressure of the politically motivated may be controlled. Such parties are not expected to influence the policies of the regime in any substantial way. Thus, in Thailand, party politics have been permitted from time to time as a means of perpetuating public order and maintaining the façade of popular control.

Obviously, in countries where repression is blatant or where political expression has once existed, the extermination of party politics may lead to disunity and the alienation of former party members from the regime. This has been true in both Syria and Iraq, where the military juntas temporarily silenced the political parties only to discover the party leaders forming opposition groups in an attempt to restore civilian government.

2. ONE-PARTY OR MULTIPARTY-PROLETARIAT STATES. [5]

Communist China
Cuba
Mongolia
North Korea
North Vietnam

On the surface, China and North Vietnam would appear to have multiparty systems, for in each case the Communist regime maintains the façade of political competition. Thus, there competed in the initial elections in North Vietnam the Democrats, Socialist, Vietnam Quoc Dan Dang (VNQDD), DHM, and a large number of "independents"; in Communist China, Communist Party members initially held only one third of the positions on the carefully picked electoral lists. In practice, however, Communists find their way into the administrations of other parties and general decisions are ultimately made by the Communist Party. Nor does the voter have a meaningful choice: the single list found at the polling booth has been carefully culled for possible opponents to Communist rule and elections are not always conducted by secret ballot. Changes brought about by the Cultural Revolution have yet to be assessed.

The "non-Communist" parties have a definite function: aside from providing a façade of competition and freedom to the rest of the world, they give the Communist leadership some indication of the thinking of outside-interest groups. More important, the multiparty concept maintains unity during the difficult transition to Communism by giving a feeling of security to non-Communist politically oriented individuals and groups and by allowing an outlet for expression not found in the one-party state. Later, a single-party system is introduced, but this concept of the "two-stage" revolution has been found relatively effective in drawing disparate groups into acceptance of the Communist regime.

3. ONE-PARTY STATES. [16]

Central African Republic: *Mouvement pour l'Evolution Sociale de l'Afrique Noire (MESAN)*
Chad: *Union pour le Progrès du Tchad*
China (Formosa): *Kuomintang*
Congo (Brazzaville): *MESAN*
Gabon: *Bloc Démocratique Gabonaise*
Guinea: *Parti Démocratique de Guinée*
Ivory Coast: *Parti Démocratique de la Côte d'Ivoire*
Liberia: *True Whig Party*
Mauritania: *Parti du Peuple*
Niger: *Parti Progressiste Nigérien*
Rwanda: *Parmehutu*
Senegal: *Union Progressiste Sénégalaise*
Tanzania: *Tanzania African National Union*
Tunisia: *Néo-Destour*

A one-party state is one in which none but the established party holds seats in the national legislature or ministries of government. The most important distinction within this category is to be found in the means by which the single party is established and maintained. In rare cases (Tanzania and Cambodia are good examples), opposition parties have been allowed to exist and to compete but have not been able to gain sufficient popular support. Democracy is accepted in principle in these states and competition is tolerated, although the scope of action of the opposition parties is usually restricted. Far more prevalent is the banning of opposition parties, the forcible co-opting of opponents, or the erection of legal or extralegal barriers to competition. Opposition parties were banned in the Central African Republic, Niger, and Gabon, while stringent measures were enforced against possible opponents in Guinea and the Ivory Coast. One-party systems may also differ on the basis of organization: some are well-disciplined systems with strong central control of members, branches, and policies; at the other extreme is found the united front, which is more nearly a loose federation of parties with differences in policy and leadership.

In most one-party states, there is little distinction between the party and the state, for the two work together to their mutual benefit. This relationship between party and government is closest in the one-party and Communist states, followed by the one-party dominant, two-party, and multiparty systems, in that order.

A central argument of one-party governments—and, in fact, a basic rationale for their existence—is the unifying and stabilizing influence they exert. Loyalty to the nation is presented as inseparable from loyalty to the party. Any efforts to sever this union are considered treasonable. The government actively promotes policies that will make the party a unifying force. Some of these policies may be instituted to destroy possible opposition; they may include the arrest of opponents, accusations of association with foreign powers, charges of election fraud or other crimes and threats concerning the possible consequences of opposition. The party may also attempt to co-opt opposition politically by explaining that there is really no place outside the organization for the ambitious politician; in states where the party has a well-developed organization and complete government support, this "explanation" is valid.

But other activities are, perhaps, more important in unifying the nation. When the government party attempts to establish branches throughout the nation, as the parties in the Ivory Coast, Guinea, and

Senegal have done, the party itself can be a powerful propaganda weapon and wield a nationalizing force. Providing a single ideology and upholding a single leader, it carries out many of the same functions as the Communist Party has in China, North Korea, and North Vietnam. Similar to Communist organizations, it is also analogous to the old party-boss system in some American cities.

The associational and welfare policies of the party also have a socializing effect. An important visitor to outlying towns in the Ivory Coast, for example, will probably be met by a member of the party's women's auxiliary, which brings the distaff side of the family into party activities. In another part of former French West Africa, he may find party-sponsored youth organizations, veterans' clubs, dramatic groups, and all sorts of associations which direct the population into the party apparatus. Like the old Tammany boss, the local party leader may also provide certain welfare aids. Or the government, in the name of the party, may give financial help to certain localities just before election campaigns are scheduled to begin. For example, Prince Sihanouk of Cambodia has been known to make contributions to township development funds from his own pocket at such times.

Finally, the central theme of the party is the necessity for unity. At election time, this theme is developed through every communication medium available. This continual emphasis on unity, loyalty, and the union of party and nation makes the national party one of the most effective means of encouraging unity in the developing world.

A word of caution is necessary, however: the single party may be united only superficially; closer inspection may reveal divisions along ethnic and religious lines. The supposedly monolithic organization may in fact be a conglomeration of associations held together loosely at the top. Zolberg quotes an observer in an Ivory Coast town:

> There is no liaison at the base among the various wards. In this sense that party, which might constitute an integrative factor for the immigrant population, provides absolutely nothing of the kind. The separateness of each of the ethnic groups is a fact acknowledged and admitted by the Africans themselves.[1]

The party may thus become only the arena for the dissension characteristic of many multiparty systems or may be vulnerable for easy overthrow.

The decade of the sixties has brought a considerable reassessment

[1] A. Zolberg, "Mass Parties and National Integration: The Case of the Ivory Coast," *Journal of Politics*, 25 (1963), 43.

of the organizational strength and loyalty of membership of the mass party systems of Afro-Asia. In a growing number of cases these parties have been overthrown by the military with surprisingly little reaction from the party membership or general populace. These organizations have included one of its prototypes, the Convention People's Party of Ghana, and the largest Communist party outside of the Communist world, the Partai Kommunist Indonesia. Even the People's Republic of China has shown the fragility of party structure and discipline as the Cultural Revolution has engendered deep conflicts within the Communist Party of China.

Several factors may be responsible for this weakness of the mass party structure. First, we may have simply misread the strength and organization of the system and taken bureaucracy and party statements and mass meetings as signs of organizational ability and popular support. The lack of reaction to the dispatch of West African parties lends support to this conjecture. Secondly, the lack of appeal may have resulted from the tendencies toward corruption, bureaucratic stalemate and efforts to build personality cults by the leader. Corruption and bureaucratic mismanagement can easily be established in the party histories of the CPP of Ghana, the AFPFL of Burma among others, while Mao Tse-tung has railed against the stultifying effect of the party bureaucracy in China. As well, personalities such as Nkrumah and U Nu appeared to have lost interest in building the party structure as they sought personal, or in the case of U Nu, less worldly goals. The result has been military takeover of one-third of the eighteen one-party systems in existence in early 1964.

SEMICOMPETITIVE SYSTEMS

1. ONE-PARTY DOMINANT SYSTEMS. [16]

> Botswana: *Botswana Democratic Party*
> Cyprus: *Patriotic Front*
> Gambia: *United Party*
> India: *Congress Party*
> Iran: *New Iran Party*
> Kenya: *Kenya African National Union*
> Korea, South: *Democratic Republican*
> Lesotho: *Basuto National Party*
> Malagasy: *Parti Social Démocrate de Madagascar*
> Malawi: *Malawi Congress Party*
> Malaysia: *Alliance Party*
> Mexico: *Partido Revolucionario Institucional*

Pakistan: *Pakistan Muslim League*
Singapore: *People's Action Party*
Uganda: *Uganda People's Party*
Zambia: *United National Independence Party*

One-party dominant systems are those in which one political party has been in power or has dominated a coalition since independence or, in the case of the Latin American states, for a relatively long period. The one-party dominant system differs from the one-party state in several significant ways: it has a higher incidence of legally and politically accepted competition; and it is found in countries where opposition parties hold seats in the national legislature or are prominent in regional legislatures. Although fraudulent activities and stern measures against the opposition have been observed in many one-party dominant countries (for example: Iran, Mexico, and South Korea), opponents have been able to survive, if not thrive. Finally, under such systems, a more distinct separation exists between party and state, although the difference in some countries—such as Mexico—may be only relative. And just as the American system remains a two-party system in spite of a rash of minor parties, so too in such states does one party remain dominant in spite of the fact that opposition parties are allowed to exist.

In a number of one-party dominant states, the major party uses the same means for maintaining unity as are used in one-party systems. Government and private machinery are used to spread the party's control throughout the nation; the leader of the party is described as the "leader" or "savior" of the country (for example: Kenyatta of Kenya and Tengku Abdul Rahman of Malaysia); and opposition parties are declared to be antinationalist and divisive. Such a system also bears inherent dangers to unity and stability, for the continuation in power of one organization leads to irresponsibility among the minority parties, who may turn toward extremism in their often fruitless efforts to dislodge the government. In democratic systems, long periods of exclusion from the government may lead to alienation from the political system itself and may encourage the growth of authoritarian ideologies among the excluded. This situation existed in Burma before 1958, when opposition groups appeared to prefer military force rather than parliamentary procedures to make changes in the government. Recently, the Alliance government of Malaysia, which has ruled that country since independence was achieved, has accused opponents of planning civil strife. In some one-party dominant states, the avenues to successful parliamentary opposition may be closed artificially and the only road left open by which minority parties may influence policy is that of extralegality. The pressures put on the opposition in Ghana left those opposed to Nkrumah with very few parliamentary methods of challenging the government.

At the same time, it should be noted that the one-party dominant system appears to be the least vulnerable to military takeover, although the party histories of Bolivia and South Vietnam show that the system is not completely stable. Perhaps the answer to this longevity may lie in the combination of the organization and leadership of the one-party system and the safety valve factor of legal opposition. Of interest is the fact that both Bolivia and South Vietnam had moved to seriously hamper opposition prior to their demise.

COMPETITIVE PARTY SYSTEMS

1. TWO-PARTY DEMOCRATIC SYSTEMS. [8]

Colombia
Costa Rica[1]
Honduras
Jamaica
Malta
Philippines
Trinidad-Tobago
Uruguay

[1] Basically a two-party state, although minor parties exist.

That rare type of political system, which most Americans have been taught is the "natural" one, involves competition between two relatively equal political parties in a democratic setting. Two-party systems are at present anything but "normal" in the developing countries. They exist in the eight countries listed above. Nevertheless, it is frankly questionable, whether the present system will last past the first postindependence elections. Similar situations in other former colonies led to a one-party or multiparty system after the end of colonial rule. The Philippines, although assiduously copying much of the American system, has not always had a two-party system. Uruguay is so advanced economically, socially, and politically that one can seriously question its inclusion as an underdeveloped state. Colombia has a peculiar system which allows an orderly exchange of power by the two parties rather than a competitive bid to the electorate. Jamaica and Trinidad are too new to allow any long-term prediction of the form their party systems will take.

Two-party competition has appeared in other countries but has usually fallen before demands for unity or the growth of factionalism within the respective parties. It seems that a democratic two-party system, with its peaceful exchange of governmental control, requires a certain forbearance, a tolerance of the opposition and a willingness to play by the rules of the game. These qualities are still rare within the countries under consideration. The success of a democratic two-party system is usually based on an agreement on fundamentals within the society. Without this consensus, the peaceful surrender of office would be unacceptable. It is easier to ban opposition in the name of unity and progress than to permit it to endanger a hard-won position of leadership.

2. MULTIPARTY STATES. [16]

Barbados	Israel
Bolivia	Lebanon
Ceylon	Nicaragua
Chile	Somalia
Dominican Republic	Sudan
El Salvador	Turkey
Guatemala	Venezuela
Guyana	Vietnam, South

(Not included in any category due to a paucity of information are Aden, former Spanish Guinea, and the Maldive Islands.)

The multiparty system is characterized by the inability of any one party to dominate the government or to obtain a majority of the seats in the legislature. Of course, there are cases in which one party with a minority of seats has been recognized as the leader of the government over long periods (such as the Mapai in Israel). However, a not always stable coalition rule is a major characteristic of multiparties in the developing world. It should be noted that the list is dominated by older states and that of the sixteen states only one is not from the Western Hemisphere or the Middle East. That state, South Vietnam, has probably the most tenuous multiparty system of all.

Students of politics have long debated the question of whether multiparty systems are a cause or an effect—or both—of disunity and political alienation. It is argued that a multiparty system implies a coalition government and that such a government results in immobilism and/or continuous flux. The example constantly cited is, of course, France during the Third and Fourth Republics. On the other hand, it is asserted that the system only reflects the basic cultural, ethnic, economic, or ideological divisions within the society, and that as long as these exist the necessary consensus for perpetuating a stable system is missing.

In the past it was argued that experiential data showed that a peaceful exchange of office was more likely to occur in multiparty systems, partly because there were no dominant organizations and because the necessity for coalition rule forced the acceptance of members of other parties. Yet, states maintaining this system have not been invulnerable to extraconstitutional change of office. In fact, the past decade has shown that the lack of consensus that multiparty systems often reflect has resulted in dangerous vulnerability to military overthrow. Of twenty-two multiparty systems in existence in 1963, nine have experienced military coups in the ensuing years. These have included older Latin American states such as Argentina, Brazil, and Peru as well as Afro-Asian "adolescents" such as Indonesia and new states such as Sierra Leone and the former Belgian Congo.

There appears to be no single variable to account for the formation of the multiparty system. Ethnic and religious variations do not explain its development in Latin American states where these factors do not primarily delineate political boundaries. Even in ethnically fragmented polities, such as Vietnam and Ceylon, the appearance of multiparty government cannot be explained in primarily ethnic or religious terms, for parties divide along other lines as well. Nor does the particular colonial heritage appear to be a decisive factor, for the list included former colonies of Spain, France, and the United Kingdom. Although seven of the sixteen states were under Spanish rule, the colonial period in these cases ended so long ago that it is difficult to draw any conclusions. One factor common to a large number of these countries is a relatively long period of independence and of experience in operating a party system. The seven Latin American states have been free for over one hundred years; Turkey has ruled herself for centuries; Lebanon and Ceylon have had considerable self-government since the 1920's; and Israel is largely ruled by people who previously lived in independent countries. The point does not include all on our list, as, for example, Barbados and Guyana.

PARTY SYSTEMS, SELF-RULE, AND STABILITY

The relationship between experience with self-rule or party activities and the existence of political competition may be tenuous, but it becomes more intriguing when one considers the following: of the eight states with two-party systems, four have been independent for considerable periods while two (Malta and the Philippines) have engaged in European-style politics for half a century or more; of the sixteen states with one-party systems, only China and Liberia have had similar experiences with independence; of the sixteen states with one-party dominant systems, only five have had party development for considerable periods.

This neat explanation breaks down when the states without effective parties are considered, for twenty-three of the thirty-eight polities in that list have been independent or enjoyed a considerable degree of autonomy for several decades. Of the twenty-three, almost two-thirds experienced a working party system at one time or another during the postwar period. Obviously, no single reason will suffice to explain the rise of a multiparty in the developing world. In most cases a unique combination of circumstances has been responsible.

The most interesting conclusion that can be drawn from this classification of parties is the high incidence of a lack of party competition. Of the ninety-eight states we were able to categorize, only one-quarter (24) display a party system in which there is a reasonable chance for a peaceful change of office. In approximately two-fifths (38) the party does not play an effective role in governmental decision-making. Five have Communist systems; sixteen have one-party systems and an equal number one-party dominant polities.

A second point worthy of consideration is the relation of political instability to the party system. This may be analyzed by relating the number of coups and serious attempts at coups in a country to the party system of that country. The period taken is that since World War II—or, in the newly independent states, that since independence. It must be remembered that a coup or an attempted coup is only one manifestation of political instability and disunity.

Chart 4-1.   Coups or Attempted Coups

System	Number of Countries	Countries with Coups
No effective parties	38	30 (79%)
Proletariat	5	1 (20%)
One-party	16	7 (44%)
One-party dominant	16	7 (44%)
Two-party democratic	8	3 (37%)
Multiparty	15	12 (80%)

The two-party systems listed in Chart 4-1 provide too few examples to allow any meaningful conclusions. Otherwise, the governments with no effective parties or with multiparty systems have the highest incidence of this manifestation of instability. Since both systems reflect a lack of political consensus, these figures are not surprising.

ARGUMENTS AGAINST COMPETITIVE PARTY POLITICS

In discussing the low incidence of competitive party systems in the developing states, consideration should be given first to the explanations offered by the countries concerned. Arguments against the establishment or maintenance of party rivalry fall into five categories, each of which will be considered in detail:

1. Political parties sabotage national unity.
2. The nationalist organization saved the nation and has a mandate to bring the fruits of independence to the people.
3. Multiple parties waste valuable time and manpower.
4. The western system of parliamentary party government does not fit local conditions.
5. Party competition is neither necessary nor natural.

1. POLITICAL PARTIES A THREAT TO NATIONAL UNITY. As previously noted, one of the major fears of new states has been disunity, and, therefore, expressions similar to George Washington's warnings on the dangers of factionalism have been frequently voiced by their political leaders. The following statement by a government official of Dahomey is typical:

> . . . The effective remedy against the evil of the party system—that division which undermines our fighting forces and plays into the hands of the enemies, who, to perpetuate our subjection, dream only of hammering any attempt we make to achieve unity—the only suitable remedy, I say, is the fusion of existing parties. . . .[2]

Thus, those seeking to establish opposition parties are often accused of "sabotaging our struggle for independence" as Nkrumah once put it. Opposition is synonymous with sedition and antinationalism, for all "right-thinking" citizens are presumably seeking the same goals.

[2] Taken from a report delivered by Alexandre Adande, entitled "In the Phase of National Construction the Fusion of Parties Becomes a Categorical Imperative," at the International Conference on Representative Government and National Progress, Ibadan, Nigeria, 1959, p. 4.

This rationale has resulted in the banning of parties in much of Africa and Southeast Asia.

2. THE "MANDATE" OF THE NATIONAL LIBERATION PARTY. New rulers readily maintain that their party has a mandate from the people arising from its success in freeing the nation from colonialism. As Nkrumah proclaimed on the tenth anniversary of the founding of his Convention People's Party:

> Comrades, it is no idle boast when I say that without the Convention People's Party there would be no Ghana, and that without political independence there would be no hope of economic salvation. The Convention People's Party is Ghana. Our party not only provided the government but is also the custodian which stands guard over the welfare of the people. . . .[3]

This position puts new opposition parties at the severe disadvantage of seeming to compete with the fathers of the country. Given the relative youth of many of the new nationalist leaders, this is no temporary hindrance to party competition. Like the first argument, it also makes the opposition appear seditious.

3. MULTIPLE PARTIES A WASTE OF TIME AND MANPOWER. A third view —the theory that the new nation is not able to "afford" a competitive party system—may find greater support among some Westerners. The bitter rivalries which arise among political opponents often mean that the members of the opposition are excluded from the administration of the state. In young nations with a notable lack of trained individuals, this exclusion can severely hinder progress. In the words of a former president of the West African Student Union:

> Thus one sees the paradox of a country which suffers from want of managerial and technological skill . . . excluding qualified citizens from service simply because they belong to a different political party.[4]

Another facet of this question is raised in the old argument that democracy is not efficient and that a state seeking rapid social and economic progress can ill afford the luxury of debate. This position has been taken by leaders throughout the developing world and has long been a rationale of Latin American strongmen.

[3] Kwame Nkrumah, *I Speak of Freedom* (New York: Frederick A. Praeger, Inc., 1961), p. 161.
[4] H. O. Davies, "The New African Profile," *Foreign Affairs*, 40:2 (1962), 298.

4. COMPETITIVE POLITICS AN INAPPROPRIATE "WESTERN" SYSTEM.

The parliamentarism in the West . . . where they hold debates and take a decision on the basis of the half-plus-one vote . . . is based on individualism. The Indonesian community is not based on individualism. It rests on the system of mutual assistance—*gotong rojong*—as members of one big family. (Sukarno) [5]

To the Anglo-Saxon in particular, or to countries with an Anglo-Saxon tradition, the two-party system has become the very essence of democracy. It is no use telling an Anglo-Saxon that when a village of a hundred people have sat and talked together until they have agreed where a well should be dug they have practical democracy. (Nyerere of Tanganyika) [6]

These two statements reflect another argument against competitive politics—the assertion that Western parliamentarism, with its demands for what Sukarno has called "free-fight liberalism when people compete for votes," is not appropriate to the new nations' search for unity and synthesis. Using arguments founded on village traditions or the lack of trained individuals in the populace, these leaders point out the "impracticality" of competition in their countries. At times, these arguments are accompanied by an expression of regret over a system tried and unfortunately found wanting. Thus, Ayub Khan, in observing that parliamentary democracy "could not work" in Pakistan, added: "Our experiences in this respect have been very sad."

5. PARTY COMPETITION NEITHER NECESSARY NOR NATURAL. Statements such as the ones already quoted lead to the final argument: that unity and cohesion are natural outgrowths of the indigenous political and social process. The argument becomes somewhat tautological at times when leaders such as Touré, Nkrumah, and Mboya of Africa and Sihanouk of Asia argue, in effect, that there is no need or desire for competition in their countries because there is no competition. "If competition were necessary and natural," they imply, "then we would have it. Since none has appeared, it must not be natural."

Not only is noncompetition "natural," it is also necessary. "A one-party government in the initial stages will be necessary for stability in Kenya," announced Mboya, and similar statements have been made by other African leaders. This philosophy is somewhat different from that expressed by most Asian leaders at the time their nations became

[5] *Times of Indonesia,* March 27, 1956.
[6] James Duffy and Robert O. Manners (eds.), *Africa Speaks* (Princeton, N. J.: D. Van Nostrand Co., Inc., 1961), p. 32.

independent. Asia's leaders at first expressed hopes for a competitive system; the one-party or no-party governments that developed are a reflection of later discouragement with the democratic process.

OBJECTIVE REASONS FOR LACK OF PARTY COMPETITION

These are the reasons given by those intimately involved in political party life, but what might be the causal elements presented by more objective observers? Some of the arguments already discussed can be established, in less emotional terms, as at least partially valid.

Although the forces behind this lack of political competition vary according to local conditions, five causative agents have been paramount. Several of these stem from the arguments already discussed: the impact of the nationalist movement and its leader; the attitudes of the ruling group and the population toward political opposition; the methods of election; the effect of long residence in office; and the existence of a different sort of competition.

1. IMPACT OF NATIONALIST MOVEMENT AND ITS LEADER. As already seen, the fact that the party in power has led the nation to independence provides it with propaganda weapons which are hard to match. By characterizing itself as the party of *Merdeka,* of Gandhi, or of the martyred Aung San, it is able to present an image compounded of past glories and future promises. Speeches, symbols—even pictures on the ballot box—are employed to remind the voter of his debt to his emancipator. A united nationalist movement that enters the period of independence as the one mass organization with political experience is able to elicit even more emotional support. This experience has been particularly vital in former French colonies, where native parties were allied to their French counterparts and politicians had the opportunity to participate in the metropolitan parliament and to view French organizational methods.

Nor can the importance of the revolutionary leader to the maintenance of party dominance be overestimated. Two factors in the new states have aided this development. First, the emotional character of the nationalist revolution has often centered on one man, and the people have come to expect their hero to give them the fruits of freedom. The party, for its part, has assiduously worked to build up the image of the leader both as a symbol of the party and as something more than mortal. Superhuman characteristics have been attributed to such men as Nkrumah and Nu. Second, the lack of education and political experience among the masses has led to an emphasis upon personalities. As one Philippine speaker noted:

An electorate unaccustomed to choosing between parties and programmes of government can only too easily be persuaded to expect everything from one man, who would solve all problems with his sincerity, energy, and personal magnetism.[7]

2. ATTITUDES TOWARD POLITICAL OPPOSITION. The leaders' comments quoted reveal a second factor responsible for lack of party competition. Where opposition is considered to threaten national unity and to endanger the goals of the revolution, those attitudes conducive to fair elections may not develop. It is not unheard of for the major party to accuse the opposition of being disloyal to the revolution and nation simply because it criticizes the new government. Nowhere was this tactic more popular than in Ghana, regarding which one writer commented:

A telling test of the extent to which parliamentary democracy is accepted by the leadership may be found in their attitude toward the Opposition in and outside Parliament. Leaders in Government and Party (CPP) appear to be unanimous in their opinion that conditions in Ghana do not require an "alternate government." [8]

This concept of parliamentary government has not been entirely missing from a number of other countries, including most of the new African states. It has led to a popular suspicion of any form of organized political competition. It is true—although not as often as Sukarno and others would have us believe—that in some societies the village political structure is established neither upon open competition—"free-fight liberalism," if you will—nor upon representative government. In some primitive societies, decisions are made as a result of discussing a problem, although no formal vote is taken. In some tribal organizations, government is somewhat similar to the Swiss *Landsgemeinde,* where problems are discussed by the entire group rather than by elected or chosen individuals. Although the number of people presently living under such systems may be relatively small, the politicians' emphasis upon this tradition has helped to turn the minds of the people against competitive politics. This view is not based upon interpretations of primitive village life alone, however, for some modern Western ideologies may be so interpreted as to deny the validity of party competition. In the words of some Burmese "socialists":

[7] Leon Maria Guerrero, "An Asian on Asia," *The Listener,* LIX (February 20, 1958), 306.

[8] Henry L. Bretton, "Current Political Thought and Practice in Ghana," *American Political Science Review,* 52 (March, 1958), 52–53.

By definition, a socialist framework means a social setting in which all forces antagonistic to socialism are nonexistent. How can therefore be [*sic*] a competition of political parties in a socialist framework? . . . Competitive socialism is indeed a contradiction in terms.[9]

3. METHODS OF ELECTION. The electoral system itself may aid the party in power. In one-party dominant systems, the fragmentation of the opposition has indirectly aided the majority party. This has been particularly true in states with the single-member district system (in a pure or modified form), under which the electoral method does not result in strict proportional representation. The best example of this is found in India, where the 1951–52 elections gave the ruling Congress Party only 44.9 per cent of the vote but 74 per cent of the seats in Parliament (a phenomenon largely repeated in later elections). Other examples are found in Cambodia, where the opposition polled 20 per cent of the votes but received no seats; Burma, where the AFPFL got only 47.7 per cent of the national vote but over 60 per cent of the seats; and Ghana, where the CPP won only 54 per cent of the votes but received over 68 per cent of the seats. It has only been where the opposition was able to unite that this electoral disadvantage has been mitigated.

Less subtle means have been used in some African states to discourage opposition. Opposition parties have either been denied a place on the ballot or have found the electoral system rigged so as to give the government party a powerful advantage. The methods of preparing party lists, and the disproportionate number of seats given to the party gaining a majority of votes vitally aids the large party. For example, the Ivory Coast has only one constituency and the voter must vote for the entire list of candidates; in Togo, parties had to line up fifty or more candidates to form a single list—and then the opposition parties were unable to get on the ballot because they had failed to submit lists "within the time set by law."

In Southeast Asia, the opposition has been harassed by similar methods. In Cambodia, members of the left-wing Pracheachon party were arrested for "conspiring with agents of foreign powers" and fourteen were executed only a month before the election. A woman who had campaigned against a government-sponsored candidate in South Vietnam at the time of Ngo Dinh Diem told the following story: upon registering her candidacy, she was "advised" by the local Governor not to run; her supporters were pressured to drop their support; her campaign posters "fell down with amazing consistency";

[9] *The Nation* (Rangoon), May 30, 1962.

she was stigmatized as a Communist; and allegedly forged Communist leaflets supporting her were spread throughout the constituency ("in spite of government security"); pressure was put on her husband; she was told that if she was elected she would be accused of violating the election law. On election day, there were efforts to set fire to election booths and, finally, the military took away a number of ballot boxes. The result was that the government candidate won, 40,819 votes to her 39,669 (8078 more votes than there were voters and 812 more than were registered—an error later corrected by eliminating some of the loser's votes).[10]

4. ONE-PARTY CAPTIVITY OF THE CIVIL SERVICE. Helping to explain such abuses is the closely related fact that very few developing states have a tradition of a politically neutral, dedicated civil service or much practice in the handling of elections. Even the hopes held for the Indian Civil Service have been somewhat dampened, while one writer stated: "All but the most unsophisticated Burmese are aware that real power rests with the political bosses." [11] This condition has often led to government use of its power and patronage to gain votes as well as to misuse electoral machinery. Examples of this abound in the developing world, as they did in our own not so remote history. Transportation in these countries is controlled, making it difficult for voters to get to the polling booth. Polling stations are placed only in progovernment areas. Opposition leaders are often arrested—either just before the election or, if they win, right afterward. Money and patronage are lavishly provided just before and during the election. The opposition is accused of subversion and antigovernment areas are warned of the consequences of "wrong" voting patterns. These activities are not universal in the developing world, but while few cases are as flagrant as—for instance—the pre-Magsaysay elections in the Philippines, some credit for continued one-party dominance must be given to the misuse of administrative power by the party in power.

5. PROVISIONS FOR COMPETITION WITHIN THE PARTY. Finally, it is a fact that competition of sorts is to be found in most one-party systems, a give and take which may be as controlled as that found in Communist states or as open as the free-for-all atmosphere of some Southern Democratic primaries in the United States. At least some type of safety valve is usually provided to lessen both the pressure of impatience from within and the effectiveness of attacks from without. The

[10] Nguyen Tuyet Mai, "Electioneering: Vietnamese Style," *Asian Survey*, 2 (November, 1962), 11–18.

[11] Hugh Tinker, *Union of Burma* (London: Oxford University Press, 1957), p. 138.

formation of a united front also allows a degree of competition. Alliances between groups which might otherwise act at cross purposes were looked upon as essential to win independence and to gain political stability in such countries as Burma, Cambodia, Malaysia, and Tunisia, as well as in the Communist states which maintain the façade of democratic government. By emphasizing the "revolutionary heritage" of the coalition, the need for unity, and the "disloyalty" of any opposition, this type of organization has often been able to last for a number of years. Its continuance does not mean that political friction and rivalry are eliminated; however, as long as the front lasts, it can both offer unity and block precipitate or radical departures from the consensus formed among the component parts of the alliance.

THE FUTURE OF PARTY POLITICS
IN THE DEVELOPING WORLD

One last question remains: What expectations can be formed of the future development of competitive party systems? According to some, history provides clues to a better understanding of the present and the future. It is certainly true that those states with greater political experience have a higher degree of party competition. But did these countries start with this sort of party structure or did they develop it from the noncompetitive political systems characteristic of the newer states?

First, the theory that time alone brings political competition is open to serious question on methodological grounds. Second, the experiences of the two-party and multiparty countries are not uniform. Most of the Latin American states originally had at least two organized political movements: the pro-Spanish and the prorebellion. The latter group was divided between those who were for revolt against Spain and those more conservative, who were alienated from the mother country when Napoleon occupied Spain. Since that time, dictators have risen and fallen, but party politics has never entirely disappeared. Most of the dictators have identified themselves with one party or another.

No pattern is to be found in the other states, except perhaps a general trend toward military rule. Some had political competition fairly early (Lebanon), while others began with one-party dominant systems (Philippines, Ceylon, Indonesia—in the early nationalist period, and Turkey). It cannot be argued that new states go "naturally" to competitive party politics. It is possible that the current political environment is such that it emphasizes unity and cohesion—particularly the Marxist concepts so popular in many new states.

If it be argued that the Latin American and Middle Eastern states have had unique political histories and only those states which have been independent for at least a decade since World War II are considered, the conclusion might be that the trend is toward less political competition. The development has been as follows:

Burma: Started with one party holding 82 per cent of the parliamentary seats; ruled by the military since 1963.

Ceylon: Started with one party holding 44 per cent of the parliamentary seats; experienced peaceful changes of government since.

Ghana: Started with a one-party dominant system, evolving into a one-party system; now under military rule.

Guinea: Started as a one-party state under Sekou Touré and remains so.

India: Has been dominated by the Congress Party since independence; Congress Party control weakening.

Indonesia: Held elections in 1954, at which time no party received a majority; later outlawed several parties and now under military rule.

Israel: Mapai won 38 per cent of the parliamentary seats after the 1949 elections and has played a strong role in a multi-party system since.

Libya: Has never established an effective party system.

Malaysia: Initially a one-party dominant system with basic Western democratic values; it remains under the control of the Alliance Party with increasing restrictions on the opposition.

Morocco: Party government has never been able to maintain itself effectively.

North Korea: Ruled by the Communist organization.

North Vietnam: Ruled by the Communist organization.

Pakistan: Parties important until 1958, when a military coup eliminated them; recently has allowed greater party activity.

Philippines: Started as a one-party dominant system; has steadily developed a democratic two-party system.

South Korea: Began with several parties, all of which became temporarily dormant when the military took power; party activity has begun again.

South Vietnam: Began as a weak one-party dominant system developing into a one-party system; following military coups, has developed a weak multiparty system.

Sudan: Began with several parties; following an interim of military rule, returned to party politics, followed by a coup.

Tunisia: The United Front Neó-Destuur Party remains in power with tightened restrictions on opposition groups.

This increasingly longer list remains small and spans less than twenty-five years, but what little evidence there is indicates no general trend toward greater political competition. Suffice it to say that past history gives scant hope for future political competition, although the experiences of Pakistan, South Korea, and Sudan show that the trend need not be irreversible.

SELECTED BIBLIOGRAPHY

Bretton, Henry L., "Current Political Thought and Practice in Ghana," *American Political Science Review*, 52 (March, 1958), 46–63.

Carter, G. (ed.), *African One-Party States*. Ithaca, N. Y.: Cornell University Press, 1962.

Coleman, J. and C. Rosberg, *Political Parties and National Integration in Tropical Africa*. Berkeley: University of California Press, 1964.

Hamm, L., "Introduction à l'étude des partis politiques de l'Afrique française," *R. jus Politique O.-Mer*, 13 (April–June 1959).

Hansard Society, *What Are the Problems of Parliamentary Government in West Africa?* Hansard Society, 1958.

Hodgkin, T., *African Political Parties*. Baltimore: Penguin Books, Inc., 1961.

Honey, P., *North Vietnam Today*. New York: Frederick A. Praeger, Inc., 1962.

La Polombara and J. and M. Weiner, eds., *Political Parties and Political Development*. Princeton, N. J.: Princeton University Press, 1966.

Mackenzie, W. and K. Robinson (eds.), *Five Elections in Africa*. London: Oxford University Press, 1960.

Mai, Nguyen Tuyet, "Electioneering: Vietnamese Style," *Asian Survey*, 2 (November, 1962), 11–18.

Padgett, L. V., "Mexico's One Party System: A Re-evaluation," *American Political Science Review*, 51 (December, 1957), 995–1008.

Schachter, R., "Single-Party Systems in West Africa," *American Political Science Review*, 55 (June, 1961), 294–307.

Scigliano, R., "Political Parties in South Vietnam," *Pacific Affairs*, 23 (June, 1960), 327–46.

Suleiman, M., *Political Parties in Lebanon: The Challenge of a Fragmented Culture*. Ithaca, N. Y.: Cornell University Press, 1967.

Weiner, M., *Party Politics in India*. Princeton, N. J.: Princeton University Press, 1957.

Zolberg, A., *One-Party Government in The Ivory Coast*. Princeton, N. J.: Princeton University Press, 1964.

V

Political Elites in the Developing Nations

The political elite comprises the power holders of a body politic. The power holders include the leadership and the social formations from which leaders typically come, and to which accountability is maintained, during a given generation. In other words, the power elite is the top power class.[1]

The new nations have experienced four broad types of political leadership over the past half-century: colonial, traditional, nationalist, and economic. In the chaos of recent events, the elites of these countries have manipulated political activities in a variety of ways.

Very generally, these states have passed through three patterns of political elite orientation. The former colonies entered the twentieth century under the rule of European colonial administrators; the independent states, under the rule of traditional elites. The colonial administrators did not always exercise unilateral control; they often worked through traditional rulers and the economic elite. This alliance was shattered by World War II, although it had begun deteriorating before that. In most new states, the new pattern—a relatively brief one—was one in which the urbanized, Marxist-oriented nationalist elite held almost complete power. Their dominance rarely lasted long after the revolution or the gaining of independence. It has generally been replaced by an intriguing combination of a more technologically oriented military with a reinfusion of traditional elements into the leadership as memories of the independence struggle wane and recognition of long-term local power relationships increases. The two groups now largely excluded from the power pattern are the old colonial elite and the economic elite, although the latter remains a

[1] H. Lasswell, *et al., The Comparative Study of Elites* (Stanford: Stanford University Press, 1952), p. 13.

force to be considered. These changes, however, have not necessarily mirrored societal changes in the countries in question.

It is important to understand the types of elites that have arisen in the developing areas—their composition, their methods of operation, and their attitudes toward nationalism, unity, and one another.

TRADITIONAL ELITES

The traditional elite comprises those who rise to leadership out of customary, hereditary, or older cultural patterns. This elite is not necessarily static, nor is it uniformly opposed to Western progress; but its power is based upon tradition, family, land, and religion. The traditional elite includes religious leaders, nobles, landowners, and people from areas given special privileges by the colonial governments. An individual member of the elite might belong to several of these categories—for example, a prince may be a religious leader or a religious leader may also be a landowner of some importance. To clarify their roles, therefore, a short description of the three major leadership groups might be in order. The examples given, however, are not intended to be all-inclusive.

1. RELIGIOUS ELITES. Religious leaders in politics may be of any faith—Buddhist, Muslim, Christian, or animist. Although the code of conduct of Buddhist monks prohibits overt political activity, members of the *sangha* (monkhood) in Burma and Ceylon have been particularly prone to enter secular politics. In Ceylon, Buddhist monks were involved in the assassination of a prime minister. In Burma *pongyis* (monks) were active in the prewar nationalist movement and took part in riots, demonstrations, and pressure-group activities during the 1961 debate over the inauguration of the Buddhist state in Burma. The religious hierarchy in both countries officially deplored these activities, but many monks—particularly the younger ones—declared that political action was necessary to gain religious ends.

Islam has never denied the close relationship between religion and politics and—although it has no official hierarchy comparable to that of Catholicism—teachers (gurus), those who maintain mosques, those who have made the pilgrimage to Mecca (hadjis), and religious associations have long been active in local and national political life. Muslim religious leaders have been particularly influential in Iran, Indonesia, and Pakistan (especially before President Ayub Khan took control). However, their national power has, in general, decreased and their influence over political matters is now primarily on the local level.

A similar fate has overtaken the Christian elites. The old Latin American triumvirate of land, Church, and army—which once ruled the countries of that continent—has been broken almost everywhere. The Catholic Church still normally takes part in conservative coalition in a number of Latin American states, but even in these cases its activities have become much more circumspect.

Finally, in primitive communities, the witchdoctor or medicine man remains a vigorous force in village decision-making, which is often left to the "supernatural." With the increase in population and the resulting increase in the pressure for land, and with the continual improvements in communications, the most primitive of these groups are disappearing. In fact, they have never wielded important or enduring influence on national politics. Astrologers, however, are still important in a number of societies, even at the national level. Major decisions—including the selection of a date for the declaration of independence, have often been made on their advice.

What areas of influence, then, remain open to the religious elite? First and foremost is the village. Except in certain states, such as Mexico and the Communist countries, which have severely restricted the numbers and activities of religious personnel, priests, monks, hadjis, and astrologers attack a wide range of problems—religious and secular. Their support for local policies, candidates, or parties is still sought in villages throughout the developing lands. Their influence tends to decline with urbanization. But as the states under consideration are—and will probably long remain—predominantly agricultural, the importance of local religious leaders appears likely to continue.

It is primarily on the national level of these new countries that the traditional religious elites have suffered their greatest loss of power. The new nationalist leaders tend to be Marxist in their orientation and secular in their tastes and tend to consider religious leadership as anachronistic and obstructive to progress. This view was sharply articulated in many new states in the first flush of independence, when the young nationalists believed old traditions could be swept away easily.

Another factor which helped to diminish the secular influence of the religious leaders was the new emphasis on sectarian differences that arose after independence. During the colonial period, there could be unity of Muslim, Hindu, or Buddhist against the Christian ruler; with freedom, however, came the necessity to define more closely the relationship between religious faith and secular goals. The sectarian divisions within the respective faiths, which had been glossed over during the struggle for independence, assumed a new importance when unity was no longer essential. Finally, the impact of Westernization, with its emphasis on science and material progress, has gradually eroded the influence of the religious elites.

Still, some areas of national politics remain subject to religious influence. Political parties—particularly those with conservative or rural interests—may seek the leadership or support of religious figures. Thus, there exist the Nahdatul Ulama in Indonesia, Muslim and Christian doctrinal parties in Lebanon, the Jan Sangh in India, the Pan-Malayan Islamic Party in Malaysia, Catholic-oriented parties in Chile and Guatemala, Muslim political organizations in northern Nigeria, and small religious associations in Senegal and other states. The role of religious leaders ranges from almost complete control of party policies and recruitment, as in the Nahdatul Ulama, to the more passive support of acceptable coalitions, as in parts of Latin America. Generally speaking, parties heavily influenced by religious leaders are a small minority in the postwar developing world.

A second avenue to national political strength involves efforts to influence particular measures being considered by the government. Although formal lobbying by religious leaders is very rare, controversial issues affecting their faiths usually bring them into open political activity. (One such issue, in the United States, is the matter of public aid to education.) In Burma, Buddhist monks influenced the government's religious education policy in the 1950's and were quite active in the creation of the Buddhist state. As Leonard Binder has portrayed them in *Religion and Politics in Pakistan,* Islamic religious leaders carried on vigorous lobbying activities for the establishment of a Muslim state in Pakistan. In Mauritania and other former French colonies in West Africa, efforts were made by Muslim leaders to infuse Islam into the state schools and to encourage the study of Arabic. Other examples abound in the developing world. The methods of exerting pressure range from talks with legislators, peaceful demonstrations, and the circulation of petitions and publications to riots. No one religion has a monopoly on any of these political tools.

A final means by which the influence of the religious elite is wielded is provided by the nationalist politicians themselves. Soon after independence, the more successful political leaders realized that their retention of power depended on effective manipulation of a variety of forces within their community—including the traditionalist, religiously oriented rural masses. This realization has led, at times, to an amusing picture: that of the secularist, nationalist politician donning —literally or figuratively—sackcloth and ashes to impress his constituents with his regard for the faith or to gain the support of apathetic or hostile religious groups. Thus, former military leader Kasem of Iraq attempted to win the allegiance of hadji associations, Nasser made the pilgrimage to Mecca, and Kyaw Nyein—a secularist Burmese politician—entered a Buddhist monastery for a while. These efforts may not be of immediate political advantage to religious leaders, but the indirect support of traditional society provided by these acts lays the foundation for future influence on the national and local scene.

In general, however, although it remains strong in some areas, the power of religious leaders has declined during the past century. As James Coleman argues in the often provocative book, *The Politics of the Developing Areas*: "Wherever the modernization process has had an impact, it has contributed to secularization, both social and political." [2]

2. NOBILITY. If the power of the religious elite has ebbed, that of the nobility has declined even more. The influence of the nobles—whether they be local chiefs, princes, feudal aristocrats, or national monarchs—has greatly diminished. None of the new black African states maintain royal families; in the Middle East, Egypt, Tunisia, Iraq, Turkey, and Yemen have overthrown their monarchs, while Iran and Jordan have made unsuccessful attempts to follow suit. In Southeast Asia, their last haven, the ruling princes are weak and are losing what little power they have. Not all ruling princes can be described as mere constitutional monarchs, however. The last vestiges of near absolute rule can still be seen in Libya, Morocco, Saudi Arabia, Ethiopia, and the South Arabian and Himalayan Kingdoms. It has been the monarchs' traditional opposition to political change that has made monarchical government such an anathema to the new nationalists in Africa and the Middle East. Modernization, nationalism, and republicanism comprise the new trinity. Although they have permitted economic development and a minimum of social modernization, those nearly absolute monarchs who survive have displayed little interest in delegating authority. Revolution, not evolution, appears to be the more probable method of future change. Nowhere in Africa or the Middle East has a constitutional monarchy been firmly established.

The powers of the local chiefs and princes also has declined. As they granted independence to their colonies, those colonial powers—such as France—which practiced direct rule appointed local chiefs (divested of firmly held religious and social ties) as administrators. As a func-

[2] G. Almond and J. Coleman, *The Politics of the Developing Areas* (Princeton, N. J.: Princeton University Press, 1960), p. 537.

tionary of the colonial regime, the chief or prince no longer com-
manded the loyalty or stature of his precolonial predecessors. The
devolution of regional local authority has been both more recent and
more traumatic in those areas which were allowed considerable local
autonomy during the colonial period. The rise of urbanized, Westernized nationalists provided a constant irritation and danger to the local
rulers, who found in them powerful enemies after independence.
However, it was obvious to many even during the last days of colonialism that the difference between the powers of the indigenous administrators under direct rule and of the ones under indirect rule was
becoming less distinct. The colonial powers, eager to carry out social
reforms or to meet economic crises, often found these rulers either
incapable or unwilling to adapt to modern ways and began more and
more frequently to bypass them.

Paradoxically, the Westernization of the regional nobles and aristocrats served to accelerate this devolution of local authority. Many of
the chiefs and nobles educated abroad became intrigued by nationalism, but often they became even more fascinated by the material advantages of the West. This draw of things Western made the more
primitive life of the countryside less appealing. The local ruler often
lost contact with his subjects by spending most of his time in the
city, or alienated them by his style of living at home. The most successful members of this class were those who could synthesize modern
concepts with the indigenous culture, thereby leading their people to
accept change in an orderly manner.

The association of the nobles with colonialism has probably been
the factor primarily responsible for the decline in their power. These
local rulers often considered the nationalists, rather than the colonial
administration, to be the chief threat to their authority and prerogatives. The nobles' fear of these young, urbanized, and often Marxist-
oriented political leaders, at variance with their own traditionalist
social views, constantly led to friction between the old and the new.
This conflict was particularly strong in areas under indirect rule;
there the local ruler not only defended his own position but also sym-
bolized regional opposition to the central government. Regional
princes, chiefs, or emirs, in areas as diverse as Nigeria, Ghana, Burma,
and Indonesia, were often actively engaged in defending regional
autonomy. This opposition was not necessarily directed against the
urban nationalists alone; in a number of cases, the antagonism was
extended to the very concept of nationalism and independence. If independence came, these local rulers argued, the regions they represented would be controlled by persons with less understanding of

their problems and less tolerance for their desire for local autonomy.

In many Afro-Asian countries, when independence did arrive, nationalist leaders—as was to be expected—insisted that the powers of local rulers be curtailed. The curtailment of these powers, however, has proceeded with caution, for these leaders still maintain considerable status in their regions. Thus, the new administrations have often eliminated local rulers by buying them off, by accusing them of a variety of heinous crimes, or by replacing them with more malleable people. Even in Ghana, where Nkrumah "destooled" a number of chiefs, the former Prime Minister declared that he was not "anti-chieftaincy":

> We are against despotic chieftaincy and are in favor of constitutional chieftaincy. But I would like to make one point clear in this connection: the chieftaincy, like any other human agency, cannot remain static; it must adapt itself to the changing conditions of the times.[3]

Some local rulers have been able to maintain a semblance of power, and for a variety of reasons. The very elections made possible by independence have led the urban elite to discover the need to seek support from regional leaders. Even when these rulers have been paid by the government to give up their formal powers, the traditional loyalty of the populace has enabled them to retain considerable political influence. It is interesting to note, for example, that in Burma, even after the Shan princes were bought off, they continued to be elected to local and national public office. In other states, compromise between regional authorities and the nationalists has been the condition for the granting of independence. This compromise has often entailed initial assurances of local autonomy—as, for example, in Indonesia and Nigeria.

3. LANDED ARISTOCRACY. The element of traditional society that is probably losing its political influence with the greatest rapidity is the landed aristocracy. The ownership of large estates by aristocratic families has not, in general, been a traditional feature of the African nations (although there are exceptions, such as Ethiopia and Egypt). This has also been true of most of the Asian nations, except the Philippines, Vietnam, and China—and in all three of these, particularly the last, the landed aristocracy no longer exerts the power it once did. Reformist governments in Iraq, Egypt, Syria, and Pakistan have made serious efforts to break up large land parcels, although their

---

[3] Kwame Nkrumah, "Movement for Colonial Freedom," *Phylon*, XVI: 4 (1955), p. 406.

progress has been slow. In Saudi Arabia and Lebanon, and particularly in Iran, the traditional agricultural aristocracy still holds considerable power. In most countries of Latin America, the economic, social, and political changes following World War II have broken the traditional hold of landed elements and the growing urban middle class is making itself heard.

In spite of their loss of position in the postwar world, the traditional elites in the developing nations have not entirely been eliminated by the new groups. In fact, after the nadir of the immediate postindependence period, the traditionalist elements are enjoying a slight resurgence. The reason is not hard to find. As one Nigerian put it:

> . . . There is another way in which the educated elite has been forced to establish closer liaison with the people in the rural areas. Since we have been having modern elections, one curious thing has happened: power has been given to the people of the rural areas through the suffrage. When elections started, large numbers of lawyers, teachers, and so on, used to go back to their villages to stand for election. To their discomfiture, not only were many of them not elected, but they even lost their deposits. . . .[4]

4. INFLUENCE OF THE TRADITIONAL ELITES. The impact of the traditional elite has been both positive and negative. The traditional elite has provided a continuing, identifiable, and generally acceptable leadership in rural areas experiencing the disruption brought about by the introduction of modern technology and the politics of independence. For example, it can be argued that it is neither Islam nor Buddhism which provides a bulwark to Communism but the religious leaders themselves, respected symbols of traditional life who see in secular ideologies a threat to their own positions. These living symbols of tradition and security in the confusion of modern life may be scorned by progressive urban nationalists, but the rural elite assert that without them there would be rural chaos. The traditional leaders who are acquainted with Western ways may provide the necessary channel for orderly change and the link between traditional and modern elites. This aid in transition has been particularly effective at the national level when the kings or ruling princes have been amenable to change or, in fact, have led it. Three such rulers are the

---

[4] Taken from a report delivered by Ayo Ogunsheye, entitled "The Traditional Order and Modern Society," at the International Conference on Representative Government and National Progress, Ibadan, Nigeria, March 16–23, 1959, mimeo, p. 6.

Sultan of Morocco, the Shah of Iran, and Prince Sihanouk of Cambodia. The first two have used their considerable power and influence to circumvent local authorities and to foster the modernization of education and public administration and the introduction of economic reforms. The Shah of Iran has been particularly active in instituting rural reforms in a country where large sections of the population are completely dominated by the landed aristocracy and religious elites. The former ruler of Cambodia, Sihanouk, voluntarily surrendered his throne in order to lead the nation's only major political party and to modernize the country (often depending on the Cambodian nobility for local leadership).

Nevertheless, more traditional leaders have tended to disrupt national unity than have attempted to encourage it. Traditional rulers tend to ally themselves with local or regional opposition to nationalist attempts to unify the country. In religious matters, they tend to emphasize communalism and intolerance toward other faiths. They have thus abetted communal friction in Malaya, Ceylon, India, Israel, Sudan, and a number of other states. In social matters, they usually support the old ways and oppose such socializing forces as national education and the establishment of a national language. Politically, the nobility were the vanguard of procolonial sentiment, for many owed their continuance in office to the colonial administration. The major divisive influence of the traditional elite has been its position as the symbol of regional patriotism and its opposition to the extension of modernizing programs designed to foster the assimilation of alienated communities.

THE NEW ELITE: CHARACTERISTICS

Paramount in almost all of the new states of Afro-Asia and steadily increasing in strength elsewhere is the "new" elite, comprised of nationalists generally characterized by their relative youth, their ties to urban and (no matter how much they deny it) Western culture, their tendency toward secularism and various forms of Marxism, and their demands for social and economic reforms. It is this elite that has tended to lead the later stages of the nationalist movement in the Afro-Asian world, to comprise large sections of the reform-minded military in Asia and the Middle East, and to form the nucleus of the rising reformist groups in Latin America. The more successful members include Sukarno, Nkrumah, Touré, Castro, Nasser, and Ayub Khan, among others—but these are only the leaders of the new class that has risen to challenge and to win the political power once held by the traditional and colonial rulers. Little detailed information on the members of the new elite—other than the top leaders—is available, but some generalizations can be drawn from the facts that are at hand. The important questions are: What are the particular characteristics of this new elite? What are its goals?

To characterize the "new elite," a comprehensive survey of the members of the leadership structure of all eighty-three states under consideration is beyond the scope of this discussion. Instead, the top leaders of the Asian and African states will be studied. The information which follows has been obtained from a survey made in 1964 of 269 prominent political personages—87 from Asia, 52 from the Middle East, and 130 from Africa. An effort was made to include all prime ministers and presidents; selected on a more random basis were cabinet members and party, parliamentary, and military leaders. The facts presented, therefore, are not conclusive and the generalizations drawn from them cannot be fully substantiated without further evidence.

1. PLACE OF BIRTH.

	Rural Area	Town	Capital	Abroad
Africa (119)	86	15	16	2
Asia (62)	21	23	15	3
Middle East (28)	4	6	12	6

A general characteristic too often attributed to members of the new elite is an urban background. Although, as will be shown, their education may have been modern, many of the Asian leaders surveyed were from small towns or rural areas and the overwhelming number of African leaders came from a rural environment. The small sample from the Middle East would appear to reflect a less mobile population. There is not sufficient evidence to support it, but a possible hypothesis is that the impact of the capital upon the person reared in a nonurban environment may be such as to propel him toward political activity. Also, many of the capitals of the new nations were more cosmopolitan than national during the colonial period, so that those reared in the capital may have been less influenced by nationalist goals. These are suppositions which need far more investigation. At present, the only verifiable conclusion is that the early environment of many Afro-Asian leaders was not normally urban in nature.

2. EDUCATION. In the entire sample, there were but six individuals with only a traditional education (one in the Middle East, three in Africa, two in Asia). Although a number of leaders received a combi-

nation of modern and traditional education, the generalization that the new elites are primarily Western-educated must perhaps be more strongly emphasized. The necessity of a Western education as a tool for political advancement has long been recognized in colonial countries, except the Muslim states. Thus, all of the six individuals who received only a traditional education were from Muslim countries where religious schools play an important role in the education of the population. In general, however, a second characteristic of the new elite is a modern education.

3. AGE.

Chart 5-1. Average Age

	On Attaining National Prominence*	In 1962
Africa	34	46
Asia	34	54
Middle East	36	55

* *National prominence*, for purposes of this discussion, is defined as election to the national parliament, the achievement of an important post in a political party or a nationalist movement, or the attainment of a high post in a civil-military administration.

Chart 5-2. Distribution of Ages (%)

PRESENT AGE

Age	Africa	Asia	Middle East
19–29	1	0	0
30–39	23	3	6
40–49	47	30	25
50–59	20	31	36
60–	10	36	30

AGE AT ATTAINING NATIONAL PROMINENCE

Age	Africa	Asia	Middle East
19–29	25	23	33
30–39	56	53	25
40–49	16	22	33
50–59	3	1	8
60–	0	1	1

Interesting comparisons can be made between the older states of Asia and the Middle East and the younger independent states of Africa. The leaders of the older states are, on the average, older. This is probably because their states achieved independence longer ago and because there has been a relative lack of political mobility at top levels in recent years. In African countries, where there is a comparative dearth of trained personnel, younger men have been able to attain prominence in recent years. The vast majority of the African leaders achieved positions of importance through participation in party activity or in nationalist movements; few arrived at these positions solely through labor union activity or participation in military or civil administrations. As might be expected, a far larger percentage of the Middle Eastern leaders attained their prominence through administrative or military posts. Asian leaders fall somewhere in between these two: a smaller percentage rose to prominence from party and nationalist organizations than is true of Africa, while the percentage that rose from the military and administrative services is somewhat larger, but not as large as that of leaders from the Middle East.

4. PARENTS' OCCUPATIONS. A final general characteristic of the leaders of the Afro-Asian World is the middle- or upper-middle-class occupations of their parents. Information on parental background is sparse, but the material that is available indicates that a high percentage of the present leaders had parents who were civil servants, traditional leaders, merchants, or teachers. A large proportion of the new elite thus came from families that had already at least partially broken with tradition. The modern education of the leaders appears to bear this out. The second largest group in the new elite came from aristocratic families and, again, Western education may provide a clue to their motivation.

The New Elite: Attitudes

What is the political-attitude pattern of the new elite? Not all these leaders have the same desires or goals, but they do share some very broad common beliefs. These include:

1. UNITY. As A. Masani, Indian party leader, once wrote, there is a desire for a common mind in a welter of different ones—for "unity in diversity," as the Indonesians would put it. Politically, this leads to the disparagement of competition among political parties and of local patriotism. Regional autonomy and federalism are rarely espoused by members of the new elite, for they see little difference between the desire for local freedom and antinationalist attitudes. The only federal state in Afro-Asia in which the states maintain real autonomy is Malaysia. Although many Latin American states term themselves "federal" in structure, it is difficult to classify them as such in practice.

These leaders are eager to spread their views throughout the nation or, more accurately, to create a nation out of the often disparate and unsocialized populations they rule. This has led them to emphasize nationalizing programs in the fields of communications, education, language, and economic development. Rural development schemes may be viewed as efforts to bring the national government to the local village and to break the influence of the traditional elites. Other programs of the new elite also have an incidental influence on their struggle for unity. Support for party government leads to the formation of local party branches outside the capital and brings about the nationalizing effects of campaigns and elections. Demands for economic and social development bring the government into closer contact with the people. The desire for international recognition leads to efforts to eliminate the more primitive areas of society in order to appear modern. Two of the earliest programs of modernization with its attendant nationalizing effects were carried out by essentially traditional elites in Japan and Thailand. In both cases, the fear of possible foreign domination and the desire to be considered equals in the world community brought economic, social, and administrative reforms which were at least partially responsible for making these two of the most unified and stable political systems in Afro-Asia. Although imitation of the West has not been quite so slavish in the postwar world, inferiority feelings engendered by what are considered primitive conditions have influenced policy throughout the developing world. Finally, the building of national monuments, stadiums, and other psychologically important —if perhaps economically unrewarding—"impact projects" have directed the attention of the nation toward the capital and its wonders. All these factors have helped to make the new elite the prime movers toward national unity in their respective states.

2. MARXISM. Although usually highly eclectic in their political philosophies, Afro-Asian leaders have been deeply influenced by varieties of Marxism. Rarely dogmatic or systematic, the Marxism articulated by the new elite is directed toward social welfare and industrialization and against capitalism (particularly foreign capitalism). But even Marxism must be adapted to the local mores and the peculiar characteristics of the respective countries. Sekou Touré expressed the sentiments of most Afro-Asian leaders when, referring to another matter, he said:

It is evident that if we impose upon a certain society structures which are incompatible with that society's conditions, its economic or cultural necessities, its perfect internal equilibrium, its means and its goals, we not only distort the man of this society but we constrain him, we enslave him, we interrupt the development and fulfillment of his faculties in peace and harmony. This is the path of assimilation.[5]

3. NATIONALISM AND ANTICOLONIALISM. It goes without saying that nationalism is an integral part of the philosophy of the new elite and one of the factors that distinguishes it from the traditional elite. This is particularly true of the idea of national unity. Not only is the new elite nationalist, but its members consider themselves the only spokesmen for that nationalism. As Nyerere once put it: "It could hardly be expected that a united country should halt in midstream and voluntarily divide itself into opposing political groups. . . ." Those characteristics of nationalism most prevalent in Africa have been nonviolence and what might be called a Mazzini-like view of internationalism. Certainly, both these aspects of nationalism have been in evidence in Asia and many Africans pay tribute to such men as Gandhi. However, leaders as different as Nkrumah and Nyerere have expressed strong support for the use of nonviolent means toward the achievement of independence. A number of African leaders have also repeatedly expressed the belief that the national state is only the first step toward some sort of international state. With rare exceptions, such as Sun Yat-Sen, Asians have been more chauvinistic.

4. ECONOMIC AND SOCIAL PROGRESS. A final characteristic of the new elite is the desire to obtain, as rapidly as possible, the economic and social development of their peoples—progress expressed primarily in Western terms. This is often tied to a desire to eliminate the last vestiges of imperialism or "economic colonialism." For example, Nkrumah charged:

> We should not be so preoccupied with the urgent problem of political independence as to overlook a scarcely less vital sphere—the economic sphere. Yet it is here, more than anywhere else, that we must look for the schemings of politically frustrated colonialism.[6]

As time passes and the first impact of independence—with its hopes and fears—wanes, closer bonds are developing between the new and the traditional elites. Each sees in the other something worthwhile. The traditionalists realize that the Western techniques of the modern elite may be valuable tools for maintaining their own power and that

[5] James Duffy and Robert O. Manners (eds.), *Africa Speaks* (Princeton, N. J.): D. Van Nostrand Co., Inc., 1961, p. 41.

[6] *Ibid.*, p. 53.

they must change lest they be overthrown by the newly educated masses. The modern elite sees the necessity of fitting its schemes and desires into the local culture if the hoped-for goals are to be attained. Thus there is developing a steady synthesis of values and techniques in the new nations.

THE FOREIGN ECONOMIC ELITE

Some mention should be made of the group which has suffered the greatest decline in power since independence: the resident foreign economic elite. This group includes the Chinese in Southeast Asia, the Indians and Pakistanis in Burma, Malaysia, and East and South Africa, and the Lebanese and Syrians in West Africa. Under colonialism, these unassimilated communities controlled much of the banking operations and rural and urban economies at the middle and lower levels. They were money lenders, bankers, rice millers, merchants, theater owners, hotel proprietors, professional men, and—in rare cases (such as Burma)—absentee landowners. Their numbers ranged from a few hundred in West Africa to thousands in East Africa to millions in Malaysia, Thailand, and Indonesia. This elite, carefully considered by Purcell, Skinner, and others, is important to this discussion in terms of its impact on the unity and stability of the new nations.

A natural antipathy between these "foreign" communities and the less affluent indigenous populations arose during the colonial period. After independence, nationalist and anticapitalist sentiment was often directed toward the forced emigration of these groups or the establishment of stringent controls on the Chinese, Indians, and "Levantines." Throughout Southeast Asia, limits have been put on the number and type of occupations open to Chinese residents. In Burma, the Chettyars were all but forced out of the country during the Japanese assault of 1941–45 and found it impossible to recoup their losses after the war. Indonesia pushed Chinese merchants out of the hinterland, although the economic chaos that followed at least temporarily led to their unofficial return. In West Africa, Middle Eastern traders have been subjected to a wide range of governmental pressures. In East Africa, Indians and Pakistanis have found it increasingly difficult to do business in spite of early nationalist promises of tolerance. Only in Malaysia and Thailand has some sort of accommodation been reached. In Malaysia—where the population is approximately one-half Malay, two-fifths Chinese, and one-tenth Indian—a potentially dangerous situation has been eased because responsible leaders of all communities believe that there must be tolerance or chaos. In Thailand, the economically dominant Chinese and the pragmatic Thai elite have agreed to divide the fruits of prosperity—a situation made possible by the less emotional nationalism of continuously independent Thailand. With these rare exceptions, however, the resident foreign elite of Afro-Asia has found itself in a radically changed position and, in some cases, in danger of losing all.

In a sense, these communities engendered disunity and instability both by their presence and by their later absence. The loss of the economic elite through government pressure gave a serious shock to the economy, particularly since the indigenous population usually had neither the training nor the temperament to take its place. In Indonesia, the Chinese who felt forced to leave bought durable goods to take with them, thus contributing to that country's serious inflation. At the same time, these communities were themselves responsible for their fates, for the pattern of their political and social views had alienated them from their adopted nations. These attitudes included:

1. COMMUNALISM. A constant complaint, heard particularly in Africa, is the lack of integration of the Asians with the indigenous population. By maintaining their own customs and religions and generally separating themselves from the nationals, these communities isolated themselves and attracted the distrust of the people. Their attitudes also reflected a certain contempt for the natives, who were neither as interested or as adept in business and the professions. In the colonial period, this communalism was often displayed in demands for separate communal voting and communal representation in government and business organizations. As independence approached, the foreign economic elite saw the inevitable necessity for cooperating with the native societies. But it was already too late: past slights were remembered and independence seemed to hold out the hope of control of the national economy—particularly that part held by foreign capitalists. The Chinese, Indians, Pakistanis, and Middle Easterners thus found themselves among the most alienated members of the nation, if they were allowed to stay in it at all.

2. POLITICAL APATHY. Basically interested in business, these foreign residents preferred to stay out of active political life except when their financial interests were directly concerned. Although this apathy tended to diminish as independence approached, the long tradition of apolitical life could not be altered easily. For example, in the 1959 federal elections in Malaya, it was reported that only 20 per cent of the Chinese eligible to register did so, in spite of the continual prompting of Chinese political leaders. Throughout Afro-Asia, this apathy

has led to an isolation from the political community at a time when nationalism has made politics a central theme in national life.

3. "POLITICAL FICKLENESS." Related to this apathy has been a willingness to support whatever government was in control, as long as it did not interfere with business. One of the jokes going about in Indonesia in former days was that every Chinese merchant had a flag for every possible government that might gain control of the Indies—Dutch, Indonesian, Japanese, English, American, and so on. Since this attitude implied acceptance and even passive support of the colonial regime, little sympathy toward the alien economic elite was to be found among nationalists after independence.

4. CHINESE LOYALTY. It is the accepted belief—accurate or not—of Southeast Asians that the Chinese owes his loyalty to China and not to the country in which he lives. This is allegedly evidenced by his refusal to accept citizenship, his trips "back home," the remittances he sends abroad, his support of Chinese education and culture, and his general support for whichever government rules mainland China. This leads Southeast Asians to believe they are harboring an unassimilable alien who owes his allegiance to a foreign power. The support for the mainland government, now that it is Communist, leads to further attacks on "subversive" and "disloyal" elements. Not all Chinese have this enduring loyalty to their homeland, but enough do to lend credence to the charges. Many Chinese leaders realize that their future lies with their adopted countries and are making stringent efforts to integrate their communities—but the suspicions of the majority endure.

Few expect any quick diminishment of the tensions among the various elites in the new states. The pessimist may point to the confusion in Indonesia or the Congo, while the optimist has viewed with pride the unique experiment in Malaysia. The major need is for a consensus on fundamentals so that at least the various groups can agree to disagree. If not, the result may be the rise of still another group: the military elite.

SELECTED BIBLIOGRAPHY

Alba, V., *Nationalists Without Nations: The Oligarchy Versus the People in Latin America.* New York: Frederick A. Praeger, Inc., 1968.

Blanksten, G., "Political Groups in Latin America," *American Political Science Review,* 53 (March, 1959), 106–127.

Butwell, R., *U Nu of Burma*. Stanford: Stanford University Press, 1963.

Dean, V. M., *Builders of Emerging Nations*. New York: Holt, Rinehart & Winston, Inc., 1961.

Halpern, J., "Observations on the Social Structure of the Lao Elite," *Asian Survey*, 1 (July, 1961), 25–32.

Howman, R., "African Leadership in Transition: A Re-evaluation," *Journal of African Administration*, 8 (July, 1956).

Johnson, John J., *Political Change in Latin America: The Emergence of the Middle Sectors*. Stanford: Stanford University Press, 1958.

Kerstiens, T., *The New Elite in Asia and Africa: A Comparative Study of Indonesia and Ghana*. New York: Frederick A. Praeger, Inc., 1966.

Lasswell, H., *et al.*, *The Comparative Study of Elites*. Stanford: Stanford University Press, 1952.

———— and D. Lerner, *World Revolutionary Elites*. Cambridge, Mass.: MIT Press, 1965.

Lerner, D., *The Passing of Traditional Society*. New York: Free Press of Glencoe, Inc., 1958.

Nkrumah, Kwame, *Ghana*. New York: Thomas Nelson & Sons, 1957.

Park, R. and I. Tinker, *Leadership and Political Institutions in India*. Princeton, N. J.: Princeton University Press, 1959.

Pye, L., *Politics, Personality and Nation Building*. New Haven, Conn.: Yale University Press, 1962.

Read, M., *Education and Social Change in Tropical Areas*. New York: Thomas Nelson & Sons, 1955.

Richards, A. (ed.), *East African Chiefs*. London: Faber and Faber, Ltd., 1960.

Schurman, F., *Ideology and Organization in Communist China*. Berkeley: University of California Press, 1966.

Segal, R. (ed.), *Political Africa: A Who's Who of Personalities and Parties*. New York: Frederick A. Praeger, Inc., 1961.

Singer, M., *The Emerging Elite: A Study of Political Leadership in Ceylon*. Cambridge, Mass.: MIT Press, 1964.

Skinner, G. W., *Chinese Society in Thailand*. Ithaca, N. Y: Cornell University Press, 1957.

Southall, A. W. and P. C. Gutkind, *Townsmen in the Making*, East African Institute of Social Research, 1957.

Van Niel, R., *The Emergence of the Indonesian Elite*. The Hague: W. Van Hoeve, 1960.

von der Mehden, F. R., *Religion and Nationalism in Southeast Asia*. Madison: University of Wisconsin Press, 1963.

VI

POLITICAL ACTION BY THE MILITARY

IN THE DEVELOPING NATIONS

In the advanced Western nations, political activity on the part of the military has usually been detrimental to the achievement or maintenance of constitutional government. Perhaps it is for this reason that intervention by the military in the political affairs of the developing nations is often decried by those who hope to see effective democratic and stable governments achieved there. The purpose of this discussion is to assess the significance of this concern against the background of the political process in the developing world. The decade since 1958 has witnessed a rash of military coups that remind the observer of the stereotype of pre-war Latin American military-civil musical chairs in the rapidity of government overthrow, if not the style of the old "palace revolution." In Asia there have been successful military takeovers in Pakistan, Burma, Laos, Thailand, South Vietnam, South Korea, and Indonesia. In the Middle East the same feat was accomplished in Turkey, Syria, Iraq, Yemen, and Sudan, to add to the long-standing military dominated government of the United Arab Republic. Even Africa south of the Sahara, most of which has been independent less than a decade, has been the scene of an increasing number of military takeovers, including Ghana, Nigeria, Mali, Dahomey, Sierra Leone, and the former Belgian Congo. In Latin America, the birthplace of our stereotype of military rule in the developing world, few countries have escaped military rule, as evidenced by post-war coups in Argentina, Paraguay, Bolivia, Brazil, Peru, Ecuador, Colombia, Venezuela, Panama, Dominican Republic, Haiti, Honduras, Guatemala, El Salvador, and Cuba.

The cold figures with regard to military coups are startling in themselves. Of the approximately 100 states under consideration, approximately 40 have experienced a successful military takeover since World War II. Half of these have experienced more than one successful coup. If we take only those countries that have achieved independence since World War II, a total of 56 states, one-third have been overthrown by the military since independence. The odds of achieving the nation's tenth anniversary without a successful coup are not quite 50-50, with three out of four nations experiencing either a successful or attempted coup. If the independence movement was accompanied by major violence (Indonesia, Vietnam, Algeria for example) odds are better than two out of three for a successful military coup. The discussion that follows, is not designed to provide an all-encompassing explanation of military politics in these areas but, rather, to point out certain instances that may call into question conventional assumptions about the political role of the military, and to analyze changing patterns of control.

TYPICAL ROLES OF THE MILITARY

The term *developing areas* encompasses lands extremely diverse in cultural traditions and social characteristics. Naturally, the political activities of the military take quite different forms in these diverse societies and appear against quite different political backgrounds. Yet a certain uniformity is apparent in the roles that the military characteristically plays. Since the end of World War II, the entrance of the military into the politics of these societies has almost always been related to major political, economic, and social changes. The political activities of the military are basically a response to the tensions connected with these developments. Whether the dominant component of change is the transition from colonialism to nationalism, or the awakening of widespread desires for a new ordering of economic and social institutions, or a combination of these, the situations that evoke military intervention in politics are remarkably similar.

It should be noted that the military is not in all instances a monolithic force. Rather, only certain of its elements have chosen to act politically. And in the characteristics of these elements there is, again, a great deal of similarity. The politically active elements come largely from the traditionally small lower-middle and middle classes—groups for which a military career is a means of achieving a more advantageous status within the social order. Many of these military leaders have spent almost their entire lives in military service, having been educated at military academies and having begun their careers immediately after-ward. Not only their training but also their association with military groups in the advanced nations provides them with relatively distinc-tive attitudes and values—one of which is an extreme consciousness of the concept of nationalism and unity. This is revealed in the writings of politically active military leaders throughout the developing world —writings in which the "national" interest supported by the military is contrasted with the "factional" interests attributed to civilian poli-ticians and to military leaders allied with dominant civilian groups.[1] Another characteristic of these politically active military leaders is an awareness of the distinction between the status of their own country and that of the advanced nations, and a resultant advocacy of "modernization," "Westernization," or "development."

These military groups, inculcated with the values of order, efficiency, and discipline, wish to see these values applied to political life. Where the army has been in the vanguard of the struggle for independ-ence, as in some parts of Asia, it may enter the political arena because of a belief that the ideals of the independence movement have been betrayed by self-seeking and corrupt civilian politicians whose factional quarrels have led to confusion and turmoil. Where reform, rather than independence, is the issue, the military often claims that it is only under conditions of stable government—such as the military can pro-vide—that the desired level of economic and social advance may be achieved.

A description of the political roles characteristically played by the military in these societies is a useful tool of analysis, so long as such a classification is regarded as a basis for comparative statements and not as an effort to establish rigid categories which ignore the diverse circumstances and the complexities of the prevailing political situation. The situations in which the military actually comes to control the political institutions of the society must be distinguished from those in which it does not directly assume power but, instead, sets condi-tions for the performance of civilian governments (as in Indonesia before 1965, Brazil, Ecuador, Jordan, Iran, Guatemala in 1944–54, and Venezuela in 1945–48). The cases in which power is actually assumed by the military can be further subdivided into those in which the military acts as a "constitutional caretaker" government—either authentically, thus voluntarily restoring power to civilians after a

[1] See, for example, Gustavo Rojas Pinilla, *Seis meses de gobierno* (Bogota, 1953), p. 72; José Lemus, *Mensajes y discursos* (San Salvador, 1957–58), I, 86; Gamal Abdel Nasser, *Egypt's Liberation* (Washington, D. C.: Public Affairs Press, 1955); *Union of Burma, Is Trust Vindicated?* (Rangoon, 1960).

limited period of time (as in Burma in 1958–60, Syria in 1951, Honduras, Guatemala in 1944, Venezuela in 1958–60, and Peru in 1956), or spuriously, refusing later to restore power to the civilians (as in Argentina and Brazil)—and those in which it takes over as a "revolutionary" or "reforming" force to carry out major changes, putting its emphasis either on the reform of political institutions (as in Pakistan) or on total social transformation (as in Egypt, Burma since 1962, and El Salvador).

1. DIRECT ACTION: THE MILITARY AS "CONSTITUTIONAL CARETAKER." Whenever it deems marked crisis, confusion, or corruption to be paralyzing political institutions, the military may seize power to carry out what it believes to be needed political reforms and to establish the conditions under which political authority may eventually be returned to a civilian government through constitutional procedures.

The first government of General Ne Win of Burma is perhaps the most striking example of the military in this "constitutional caretaker" role. In 1958, Burma was near civil war as a result of a split in the AFPFL, the united front party that had governed the country since the achievement of independence in 1948.[2] On the "invitation" of Prime Minister U Nu, General Ne Win assumed power and initiated a general housecleaning. Corrupt politicians were fired (some were criminally prosecuted), insurgency was greatly reduced, courses in village democracy were established, the streets of Rangoon were beautified, and price control was instigated. Almost every area of national life experienced the effects of the military's efforts to reform the nation. Ne Win had first promised to hold national elections in six months; this waiting period was then lengthened to eighteen months, but at the end of that time Burma held her freest elections since independence and the army voluntarily relinquished its governmental burdens. Although there is little doubt that the army was frequently highhanded or that the civilian population resented the sacrifices demanded of it, there is no denying the material progress or the free elections brought about by the military. The return of the military in 1962 was of a different type and, perhaps, shows that control may be difficult to surrender permanently.

Less clearcut than the case of Burma was the military's entrance into Turkish politics in 1960 (although Kemal Ataturk has been the model for the leaders of several military "caretaker" governments). That army intervention in Turkish political life was made necessary

[2] For two views on the split and resultant army rule, see Sein Win, *The Split Story* (Rangoon, 1959), and *Is Trust Vindicated?* (cited in note 1).

by student riots and the oppressive measures by the Mendares government is doubted by more than one observer.[3] Prior to the takeover by General Cemal Gursal, the army and the civilian government had maintained a mutually useful partnership, with the military responsible for the program of general development. There is evidence that the coup was not entirely devoid of personal animosity caused by disappointments in the matter of promotions and by political bias against the ruling Democratic Party. Needed reforms in the legislative, judicial, and representative systems were achieved and Turkey appears to have returned to civilian rule.

In Honduras, postwar progress toward stable civilian government in a land with a stormy political history was interrupted by the oppressive regime of Julio Lozano Diaz. This government was overthrown in 1956 in a coup led by junior officers. A military junta was established; it ruled Honduras for one year, then held elections (in which the military did not participate) for a constituent assembly and returned Honduras to civilian rule. Of course, the military continues to be a prominent political factor in this nation, but its political activity is becoming increasingly discreet. Similarly, in Guatemala in 1944, younger officers assisted students and middle-class groups in the overthrow of the dictatorship of Jorge Ubico, and established conditions for the election of a civilian president. The army remained rigorously neutral during the campaign.

In Venezuela, the defection of the navy and the air force led to the collapse of the Perez Jimenez military dictatorship in 1958. The leading member of the junta established a "caretaker" government and ran for the presidency in elections administered by the junta. He was defeated by a civilian politician, and retired from political activity. Peru found itself in a state of acute political crisis in 1948, when the long struggle between the radical APRA party and the traditional conservative forces culminated in the virtual breakdown of the only authentically civilian government in many years. In response to this situation, Colonel Manuel Odria staged a military coup and took power. Conservative forces were at first elated, for they looked on Odria as one of their own, but it soon became apparent that he would restrict the activities of conservative as well as APRA political forces. Odria ruled Peru for eight years. In 1950, he "legitimatized" his rule in a controlled election. But in 1956, at the end of his term,

[3] An interesting exposition of the Turkish situation may be found in David Lerner and Richard Robinson, "Swords and Ploughshares: the Turkish Army as a Modernizing Force," in *World Politics*, 13 (October, 1960), 19–44.

he called for national elections, left the nation a few days before they took place, and looked on from abroad as his handpicked candidate was firmly defeated.

There is, of course, a great distinction to be made between Ne Win's Burma of 1958–60 and Odria's Peru. In Burma, the military entered politics diffidently and ruled without violence. Odria came to power in the tradition of the Latin American military coup and ruled in an often brutal and oppressive manner. In Burma, the military stayed in power for only a few months; in Peru, it ruled for eight years. Yet in both instances the military served to stabilize a chaotic internal situation. In both cases the military stepped down after a prescribed period of time. In neither case did the military leaders blatantly use their power for personal economic aggrandizement.

In the instances described above (with the possible exception of Turkey), the military actually dealt with the crisis that occasioned its seizure of power, and restored civilian government after establishing the conditions it deemed essential to effective civilian political control. It is essential to note, however, that in many situations where the army has justified its rise to power as the "constitutional caretaker" and has been widely applauded for its assumption of this role, the appeals and benefits of power have seemed to be overwhelming— perhaps confirming Lord Acton's famous dictum—and the military has been loath to surrender control to civilian politicians. In fact, there appears to be an increasing tendency for the military to remain in power for longer periods and to return to control after varying periods of civilian rule. As noted earlier, approximately one-fifth of the states of the developing world have experienced more than one military coup since World War II. In Brazil and Argentina the army apparently plans to remain in control of the decision-making apparatus for some time to come. In Africa, primary military influence on the governmental process appears to be more than temporary in Ghana, Nigeria, and the Congo (Kinshasa), and recent coups in the former French colonies do not seem to have broken the pattern. The Middle East has witnessed recurring coups in Syria and Iraq as well as increasing military influence in Lebanon, Jordan, and Israel because of the international situation in the area. Asia provides a mixed bag of diminishing military influence (but continued importance in civilian affairs) in Pakistan, South Korea, and South Vietnam as well as seemingly long-term domination in Burma and Indonesia.

A further pattern is developing: There has been a tendency in Afro-Asia, comparable to earlier Latin American experience, for the military leader during the coup period to stay in power as the elected head of the succeeding civilian administration. Paramount examples have been Gursal of Turkey, Park of South Korea, Thieu of South Vietnam, and Park of South Vietnam. The leader may literally don "civies" and resign his formal military role or he may remain both military commander and head of the civilian administration.

A paradoxical twist to this situation is evident in the case of Colombia. There, in 1953, after five years of violent civil war, the army intervened in political affairs—for the first time in over fifty years. Although the regime of General Gustavo Rojas Pinilla was at first widely supported as a solution to the bitter conflict between the Conservative and Liberal parties, disillusionment quickly set in when it became apparent that Pinilla was determined to stay in power and to reap the maximum advantages of political control. Ironically, however, his government did contribute to the achievement of political stability in Colombia, for—in order to effect its overthrow—the Liberal and Conservative parties reached a reconciliation, on the basis of which civilian government was restored.

2. DIRECT ACTION: THE MILITARY AS SPEARHEAD OF REFORM OR REVOLUTION. When the military acts as "constitutional caretaker," it generally does not try to effect any basic changes in the structure of political institutions. Rather, it regards its role as that of establishing the conditions within which existing constitutional arrangements can be made effective. This situation is to be distinguished from those in which the military assumes power and endeavors to create new political institutions that, in the long run, will provide for effective civilian government. The program of "basic democracies" undertaken in 1959 by the Ayub Khan government in Pakistan is a notable case in point. After banning parties and parliament, the new military government systematically restructured political institutions from the village level up. Under the Basic Democracies Order of 1959, a five-tiered system was established in order to provide the populace with experience in voting and administration. Pakistan's first nationwide elections were held for 80,000 representatives to the multivillage Union Council. The government next sought the election of a national assembly and the formation of political parties. As in Burma, economic and social reforms have been extensive.[4]

Closely related to this political role of the military, yet clearly distinct from it, is the situation in which the military government seeks to effect a basic economic, social, and political transformation

[4] See Harry Friedman, "Pakistan's Experiment in Basic Democracies," *Pacific Affairs,* 33 (June 1960), 107–25.

of the society. The military becomes a revolutionary movement in itself, with an ideology and a program for large-scale social transformation. In most instances, the political intent of such a regime is identical with that of the military government in Pakistan; in addition, however, it is assumed that effective civilian government will not be possible until the basic economic and social prerequisites of democratic government have been established.

The regime of Gamal Abdel Nasser well illustrates this type of military role. The military forcibly entered the Egyptian political scene to establish the social, economic, and political reforms needed as preconditions for democratic government. Land reform, the acquisition of the Suez Canal, and a general development of the economy and social services followed. Yet the coup occurred in 1952, and democratic institutions are still largely lacking. "We have already declared," said General Naguib in 1952, "that our principal aim is to establish a 'true democratic government' in Egypt. If political parties will become perfectly reorganized by February 1953, elections will take place at the fixed time, and without undue delay." But by 1954, General Nasser was stating that "Egypt needs social and economic strengthening by authoritarian methods and political purge . . . before a democratic constitution." [5] In Egypt, the army—instead of developing into a "caretaker" or temporary reforming force—became and remained the chief revolutionary power. The most far-reaching economic and social changes promulgated by the military has taken place in Burma since the coup of 1962. The army not only eliminated political parties, the constitution, the federal system and the parliament, but also set out to revolutionize the economic system under the banner of "The Burmese Way to Socialism." Some 168 industries were nationalized, as were many small businesses; middlemen were eliminated in the agricultural sphere; and the state quickly took over the economy. Major changes were also made in education. Another comparable situation existed in 1948–60 in El Salvador, where the governments of Oscar Osorio and José María Lemus attempted to effect a moderate social revolution under military auspices as the most viable alternative to a more radical manifestation of social discontent.

3. TACIT COERCION: THE MILITARY AS BACKER OF CIVILIAN GOVERNMENT. The second major category of the political roles of the military includes those cases in which the military does not directly assume power but remains as a major factor in the political environment,

[5] K. Wheelock, *Nasser's New Egypt* (New York: Frederick A. Praeger, Inc., 1960), pp. 19, 36.

setting the conditions for the performance of civilian governments. Situations of this kind can be found in a dozen nations, with numerous variations.

In Indonesia, the military—which for two decades supported the government of Sukarno—was, in effect, lending its weight to a regime led by an independent national civilian leader and seeking to bring a measure of stability to an extremely factionalized domestic political situation. After 1965 it gradually deposed Sukarno and took power. Recent events in Brazil provide an outstanding illustration of this military role. The surprise resignation of Janio Quadros and the impending succession of Joao Goulart, whose radical inclinations were much distrusted by moderates and conservatives, threatened to plunge Brazil into political turmoil. As it has done many times in Brazil's history, the military stepped in to create a *modus vivendi* which gave at least temporary satisfaction to the rival factions, but by 1968 it appeared to have taken a more permanent role of chief decision-maker. In the Dominican Republic, after the assassination of Rafael Trujillo, the military seemed consciously—through its support of the Balaguer government—to be attempting to keep the lid on a potentially explosive domestic situation.

In Ecuador, from the late 1940's the military supported a succession of constitutionally elected civilian governments; within a historically tumultuous political framework, it acted to ward off the recurrent threat of insurrection. Similarly, in the Philippines the military intervened in 1951 to protect the integrity of the electoral process, but remained primarily apolitical. In Jordan and Iran, the army has been the mainstay of government elites not universally accepted by the population, and the constant threat of a coup has given it a powerful voice in the councils of state. In Guatemala in 1944–54 and in Venezuela in 1945–48, members of the junior officer corps supported "social democratic" movements, enabled them to come to power, and assisted in the consolidation of their rule. But in all such cases, the relationship between the military and the civilian government tends to be highly fluid, and the fear of army coups can be a divisive rather than a stabilizing factor. It should also be noted that in situations such as those occurring in Laos, Jordan, and Iran, the use of the word *reforming* to describe the role of the military is open to question.

It is thus possible to abstract, from the heterogeneous conditions and cultures of the developing Afro-Asian and Latin American nations, typical patterns of the political roles played by the military, and such classifications are useful for purposes of comparative analysis. However, if the implications of these paterns are to be fully understood, they must be considered within the particular national environments.

MILITARY INTERVENTION IN AFRO-ASIA

An assessment of the significance of the military's entrance into hitherto prohibited areas of civilian government in the Afro-Asian states must take into account the fact that independence has come but recently to most of these nations. The importance of this fact is clear when nations with histories of independence or autonomy—such as Iraq, Iran, Egypt, Jordan, Thailand, and Turkey—are compared with those that have gained freedom since World War II—such as Pakistan (1947), Burma (1948), Indonesia (1949), Laos (1954), South Vietnam (1954), Sudan (1956), Ghana (1956), and the rash of African states achieving independence and their coups since 1960.

Independence was thought by many newly free peoples to be the beginning of the millennium. To be sure, there were some intimations of difficulties—but at least implied in the declarations of nationalist leaders was the belief that a country run like hell by the indigenous population was preferable to one run like heaven by a colonial administration. But the myth of freedom demanded that social, economic, and political progress quickly follow independence. And under the civilian politicians, this promise was not fulfilled: Pakistan, Ghana, and Sudan suffered from corruption, division, and maladministration; Burma foundered under twelve years of revolts, interparty strife, and administrative ineptitude; Indonesia never achieved the unity proclaimed in her national motto and faltered economically in spite of the numerous panaceas offered by Sukarno; Laos, South Vietnam, Nigeria, and the Congo were racked by internal warfare.

Under these conditions, the army began to reconsider the purely military role it had held during the colonial period: Burma, Pakistan, and Sudan came under army control in 1958; the government of Laos was taken over by the military during the next year; civilian government of the Congo Republic lasted only a few months; the military deposed and allegedly assassinated Ngo Dinh Diem in South Vietnam in 1963; then came a rash of coups in Africa as Nigeria, Dahomey, Sierra Leone, Ghana, Mali, and Algeria were among the new African states to suffer coups in the first decade of their independence.

The publicly announced reasons for these intrusions displayed a remarkable similarity. General Mirza, who with Ayub Khan led a successful coup in Pakistan in 1958, claimed:

> I saved the country from a disaster which would have been bloody revolution. . . . It has so many dangerous compromises that Pakistan would disintegrate internally if the inherent sickness were not removed.

To do this, he proposed "to get twenty to thirty good clear chaps together to draw up a new constitution," which—at some future date—would be subject to popular referendum. General Abboud of Sudan promised:

> In changing the prevailing state of affairs, we are not after personal gain, nor are we motivated by any hatred or malice toward anyone. Our aim is the stability, prosperity, and welfare of this country and its people.

The army in Burma reiterated these declarations but became somewhat more poetic when it compared its activities to those of Hercules in cleaning the Augean stables. However, these self-portrayals present an incomplete picture of the political and social milieux that instigated the armies' break with their apolitical traditions.

In most cases, these newly independent states have been racked by internal or external conflicts that have demanded continuous military alertness. Pakistan has been bedeviled by the problems attendant on partition, Kashmir, and the Afghan border. Burma has since 1947 faced revolts by the White Flag Communists, the Red Flag Communists, PVO forces, the Karens, the Shans, and the KMT. Indonesia has been plagued by insurrections in the outer islands as well as by conflicts with the Dutch over West Irian and the Malaysians over Borneo. The Laotian government has been the victim of a grim game of political musical chairs. And the Congo, Nigerian, and Vietnamese crises need no elaboration. As a rule the African states have not found this factor vital.

These conflicts are doubly significant in explaining the frustration and dissatisfaction of the military. First, the army—almost exclusively involved in military operations—was not tainted with the corruption and maladministration charges leveled at the civilian government; thus it appeared to be the reasonable alternative to the faltering politicians. Second, some members of the military undeniably felt that their operations in the field had been impeded by the ineptitude and bickering of the civilians. It was believed that efficient military control could more quickly solve other conflicts in which the army was involved. In Pakistan and Korea, this presumption proved to be correct.

Although other factors must be emphasized, that which usually triggered army intervention was the deterioration of the civilian governments to the point at which civil war—or at least bloodshed—threatened. In Burma, the split in the AFPFL, which had ruled the country since independence, had produced a real danger of civil war when General Ne Win stepped in. In Indonesia, Nasution gained considerable stature after the series of revolts in the outer islands during 1958. Among the reasons given by Mobutu for his gamble for power in the Congo was the fear of further bloodshed.

Yet these factors do not sufficiently explain why the army was the chief alternative to the faltering politicians. Several facets in the social and political life of these nations appear responsible for this choice. First, the educated group from which political leadership is drawn is pitifully small and therefore provides only a small reserve of new leaders. Second, the economic life of the nation is usually in the hands of nonindigenous elements; in fact, in many of the states, the people view commerce as a profession with disdain. However, the party bureaucracy has tended to keep aspiring young people from winning positions in the civilian government, making the army the only road to status, power, and the achievement of personal and national social and economic gain. And when the civilian politicians prove unable to cope with the problems of independence, the army takes over.

The background of the military leadership is another reason why the army is the chief alternative. The military elite of the states under consideration can be divided into two groups: those who participated in the nationalist movements and were politically oriented (as in Burma, the Congo, Vietnam, and Indonesia); and those who were primarily apolitical professional soldiers (as in Pakistan, Sudan, Nigeria, Ghana, and the former French black African states). In the first instance, the army could present itself as the "true" and "unsullied" heir of independence—the one sector of the nationalist movement unblemished by corruption and maladministration. The second group could portray itself as the apolitical and unselfish protector of the national interest, pointing to its former military record as confirmation.

In the older Afro-Asian states (Egypt, Iraq, Iran, Jordan, Thailand, and Turkey), where the military has intervened in political life, similar factors are found. In the Middle East, the Arab-Israeli dispute led to bitterness and frustration with the corrupt and inept civilian governments of the Arab nations. Turkey almost fits within the category of newly independent states because of the effects of Ataturk's revolution. In all these states the military class developed as part of the small, educated elite. Yet the absence of the distinctive milieu that surrounds the winning of independence makes an important difference between the political role of the military in the newly independent states and that of the military in the older states.

As has been mentioned, independence was regarded in the new states as the gateway to Utopia. In Cambodia, many thought it would mean the elimination of taxation, "a French invention." One concept suffused all the postwar nationalist movements: the ideal of democratic institutions and processes. This has usually remained only an ideal, for reality has brought disillusionment; but each new government has, of necessity, accepted the ideal. Acceptance has not always led to parliamentary democracy in the Western style, but neither has it usually led to prolonged military dictatorship. Thus, in some of the new states, the military has remained apolitical while in others it has refused to take that last step toward overt control. When it has taken control of the apparatus of the state, it has until recently promised a return to democratic rule (Sudan, Pakistan, the Congo, South Vietnam, and Ataturk's Turkey). But in the older states, where this democratic idealism was never as strong, or has waned, the military has not been subject to the same pressures to return power to the civilians and has often either remained in power (Egypt) or surrendered power to the civilians for only short periods (Iraq and Syria). In some states, of course, still another situation has arisen, in which the absence of demands for democratic institutions and processes permits the military to enter a struggle for power without ideological considerations. This development is exemplified by Thailand, where reform is a minor factor in military coups.

The older states are likely to have built up a bitterness toward civilian governments, and therefore to be disinclined to reinstate them when the military has taken control. In the new nations, the civilian politicians and the military leaders may have been comrades-in-arms during the nationalist movement; in the older nations, politicians may be castigated as corrupt landlords and merchants who have milked the people and deprived the army of victory in the field. It should be recognized that in the old states, unlike in the new, the economic elite may be indigenous and a controlling element in the civilian government or, as in Thailand, in league with the political elite. The radical economic reforms actually carried out by the military in states such as Egypt and Iraq further hinder a return of the instruments of power to civilians. Thus, in the older nations, the army—when it has entered political life—has tended to remain a permanently powerful group, unwilling to relinquish control.

MILITARY INTERVENTION IN LATIN AMERICA

In Latin America, unlike in the Afro-Asian world, the entrance of the military into political affairs is not primarily related to postwar events. There, the military has a long tradition of political activity— dating to the wars of independence of the 1820's and 1830's. But political and social changes of recent years have had a significant effect on the military's role in the developing areas of Latin America.

The postindependence governments established by military leaders in these nations bear striking resemblances to those established in the newly independent nations of Africa and Asia. Such figures as Bolivar, San Martin, and Santander conceived their role as one of holding power until civilian political leadership was capable of taking command. Unfortunately, however, the small sector of the civilian population that could have provided effective government was unable or unwilling to do so. Military leaders seized the opportunity to fill the void left by the failure of civilian political groups and used their power for their own advantage. Lieuwen's discussion of this tradition in Venezuela might well apply to most of the Latin American nations under consideration:

> During the early nineteenth century, this military intolerance of civilian rule did not represent selfish praetorianism. The army at first considered that its role lay in filling a political vacuum until such time as responsible civilian parties emerged. But with the passage of time . . . the patriotism characteristic of early military rulers . . . began to wane. . . . Venezuelan politics were virtually reduced to a battle between competing factions of the armed forces.[6]

The rule of the military or paramilitary *caudillo* or strongman became the characteristic form of political leadership in nineteenth- and early twentieth-century Latin America. For many of these nations, the alternative to perpetual factional rivalries—military or civilian— was the assumption of power by an exceptionally capable or brutal *caudillo*. The histories of many Latin American nations are character-

[6] Edwin Lieuwen, "Political Forces in Venezuela," *The World Today,* 16 (August, 1960), 345.

ized by the alternation of periods of chaos, with periods of dictatorship. In general, throughout the nineteenth and early twentieth centuries, the military supported the dominant civilian groups. Although some of the great *caudillos* carried out large-scale internal improvements, few made efforts to modify the semifeudal nature of the economic and social order. The alliance of the military with the economically dominant group is not, of course, surprising. The interests of the two groups were complementary, though not identical: the military sought power for wealth and prestige; the civilian elites supported these ambitions in exchange for assurances that their own privileged position in the social order would not be disturbed. There was, in fact, no alternative course for the military to pursue toward its objective. The forces seeking a revision of the existing order were either nonexistent or politically inconsequential.

During the first decades of the twentieth century, growing political awareness and the rise of the middle class presaged changes in the political balance of these societies. In World War II, one aspect of hemispheric defense policy involved assuring the stability of incumbent regimes; therefore, a moratorium on the adjustment of existing power relations prevailed throughout Latin America. But with the end of the war, the implications of the forces for change suddenly became clear. New political movements, seeking a thoroughgoing revision of the existing economic and social system, became prominent contenders for political power. To the masses of followers they attracted, they held out the promise of a "social revolution." The strategy of those military leaders who entertained political ambitions now became more complex: formerly, they had held essentially the same economic and social philosophy as the factions of the small elite; now their response took a variety of forms.

Factionalism has long been characteristic of the Latin American military, as individuals and cliques have pursued their own advantage in politics. With the development of conflict between social-democratic and conservative forces in the years after World War II, military factionalism took on a fairly distinct pattern. The high-ranking military officers generally maintained their alliances with the historically dominant groups and sought to suppress the new political forces. In many instances, however, the junior officers identified more closely with the middle-class leadership of the social-democratic movements than with their military superiors. Various factors—the nature of their education, their contact with the advanced nations, their social aspirations, and their middle-class background—brought their objectives closer to those of the new political forces.[7] In Guatemala, El Salvador, Honduras, and Venezuela, defections by junior officers played an essential part in bringing the new political movements—led by the middle classes—to a share in political influence and authority.

But although the junior officer cadres often enthusiastically identify with the policies of their middle-class allies, their actual support remains contingent on the protection and enhancement of the historic prerogatives of the military. The military is, in effect, adapting its political role to the conditions of a new political era. In Venezuela in 1945, for example, elements of the junior officer corps supported the bid for power of the social-democratic party, Acción Democrática. A military coup was staged and the incumbent government overthrown. The alliance endured until the new Acción Democrática president, Rómulo Gallegos, intimated that the regime favored a more limited military organization in Venezuela. The military's response was swift: the same officers who had supported Acción Democrática in 1945 overthrew it three years later.

Though in some cases the military may adjust to the new era of Latin American politics by allying with the rising political forces, in other cases it may support its political ambitions by attempting to resolve the conflict between conservatives and reformers over the proper course to be taken in achieving economic development and social reform. The policies it advocates in this situation are in fact an adaptation of those of the great *caudillos*. The military undertakes to provide internal stability and order, efficient administration, and the essential prerequisites of development and reform; it will be guided not by "exotic formulas" but by "scientific and technical norms"; it will place "concrete achievements" above "grandiose plans." [8]

The slogan "Peace and Progress" has inevitably been used to justify military governments in Latin America. With no attempt to defend the oppressive political tactics of such regimes as those of Batista in Cuba, Trujillo in the Dominican Republic, and the Somozas in Nicaragua, it must be recognized that the widespread, recurrent, and persistent support that the military has received when it has assumed such a political role in Latin American countries lends an air of

[7] Interesting dircussions of this "new role" of the military are contained in Edwin Lieuwen, *Arms and Politics in Latin America* (New York: Frederick A. Praeger, Inc., 1960), and John J. Johnson, *Political Change in Latin America: The Emergence of the Middle Sectors* (Stanford: Stanford University Press, 1958).

[8] See, for example, Lemus and Rojas Pinilla (both cited in note 1); Junta Militar de Gobierno, *Un año de gobierno* (Tegucigalpa, 1957); Manuel Odria, *Principios y postulados del movimiento restaurador de Arequipa* (Lima, 1956).

validity to its accusation that civilian leadership has failed to provide effective government.

It sometimes seems that the military's role as a potential "constitutional caretaker" is implicitly or explicitly recognized as a functional part of the political system of Latin America. In some situations, the military seems to be the acknowledged interpreter of the constitution. Thus Article 176 of the 1946 Brazilian constitution notes that "the armed forces are intended to defend the nation, and to guarantee the constitutional powers and law and order"; Article 177 observes that the ministers of war, navy, and air are "under the supreme authority of the President of the Republic within the limits of the law." Passages in a somewhat similar vein are to be found in the constitutions of other nations: El Salvador (Articles 142, 143), Dominican Republic (86), Guatemala (149), Haiti (153), and Peru (213). On the other hand, the possibility that the military will act in a "caretaker" role is sometimes explicitly prohibited by the constitution, as it is in Ecuador, where Article 155 provides that "Only the issuing authorities will be responsible for orders manifestly contrary to the constitution and laws." Latin American military leaders, in their own writings, often stress as one of the military's most important social roles its obligation to "defend" the constitution against "infringement" by civilian authorities. In Honduras, for example, the military "will assume the irrevocable function of permanent guarantors and zealous keepers of the integrity of the nation's institutions," and in Colombia, "the armed forces will continue to be the insubornable guardians of the democratic maintenance of our institutions." [9]

Also a long-established part of the Latin American political system is the military's background role in setting conditions for the activities of civilian governments. The possibility of action by the military in defense of its own interests or of the interests of the groups with which it is allied must be accounted for in the political strategies of all who would win and retain power in most Latin American nations. Victor Alba expresses the liberal's discontent with this state of affairs:

> Must a ministry be changed? Careful, the army would be disturbed. Should the salaries of the miners, or the banana or oil field workers be raised? Watch out, because the companies will negotiate with the military. Is it necessary to promulgate an agrarian reform law? Don't even speak of it, for the landowners have influence with the army.[10]

[9] See Rojas Pinilla and Lieuwen (cited in notes 1 and 7).
[10] "El militarismo en la historia de Iberoamerica," as published originally in *Combate*, 1 (July–August, 1958), 7.

Historically, as Alba suggests, this role of the military has generally served to restrain the forces seeking revision of the existing order. Today, however, the possibility of military restraint must be taken into account by conservative as well as by radical forces, as was forcefully demonstrated by the recent intervention of the military in Ecuador to bring to power the quite radical Carlos Julio Arosemena, although it later helped to depose him.

The Military in Politics: An Evaluation

All this would indicate that the political role of the military in the developing areas is not adequately analyzed by the simple characterizations currently employed in many scholarly studies as well as in popular works. Too often, military intervention in the politics of these nations is dismissed as "military dictatorship" or rule by the "military strongman" without a full inquiry into the nature and dynamics of the political systems within which these phenomena appear. At times, such events are viewed in terms of the comic-opera palace coup—a model derived from nineteenth-century events in Eastern Europe— and evaluation is limited to the norms and standards prevalent in the constitutional democracies of Western Europe and North America.

If these nations are truly regarded as developing areas searching, amidst a multitude of contemporary circumstances, for effective political institutions appropriate to life in the twentieth-century world, the role of the military in their political affairs may be seen in a new light. Without condoning the blatant excesses in the use of military power that have occurred and will continue to occur in the developing areas, this discussion has endeavored to point out some of the instances in which the military has acted as a force for political stability or reform in regions where no other sectors of society seemed able or willing to provide either. In Africa, Asia, and Latin America—where low levels of political awareness and lack of experience conspire to limit the numbers of potential leaders available for the difficult and complex tasks of modern government—the military, almost of necessity, may come to play a major political role.

But military politics in these nations can be regarded as only a temporary solution to political problems. It represents a condition that exists to be transcended, and it is justifiable only in these terms. Perhaps the experience of Latin America will prove instructive for the younger nations of Africa and Asia. The vacuum left by the failure of Latin American civilian sectors to develop a viable alternative to the military governments after the wars of independence has invited the constant and sometimes irresponsible intervention of the military in political life. Unless civilian elites in the developing areas make use of the respite from crisis that occurs when the military assumes a stabilizing or reforming role, they may indeed reap the whirlwind inherent in government by the military.

SELECTED BIBLIOGRAPHY

Alba, Victor, "El militarismo en la historia de Iberoamerica," *Combate*, 1 (July–August, 1958).

Fischer, S., *The Military in the Middle East*. Columbus, Ohio: Ohio State University Press, 1963.

Fluharty, V. L., *Dance of the Millions: Military Rule and Social Revolution in Colombia, 1930–1956*. Pittsburgh: Pittsburgh Press, 1961.

Huntington, S., *Changing Patterns of Military Politics*. New York: The Free Press, 1962.

Janowitz, M., *The Military in the Political Development of New Nations*. Chicago: University of Chicago Press, 1964.

Johnson, J., *The Military and Society in Latin America*. Stanford, Calif.: Stanford University Press, 1964.

——, *The Military in the Underdeveloped Areas*. Princeton, N. J.: Princeton University Press, 1962.

Khadduri, M., "Role of the Military in Middle East Politics," *American Political Science Review*, 47 (June, 1953), 511–24.

Lerner, David and Richard Robinson, "Swords and Ploughshares: the Turkish Army as a Modernizing Force," *World Politics*, 13 (October, 1960), 19–44.

Lieuwen, Edwin, *Arms and Politics in Latin America*. New York: Frederick A. Praeger, Inc., 1960.

——, *Generals* vs. *Presidents: The New Military in Latin America*. New York: Frederick A. Praeger, Inc., 1964.

McWilliams, W., ed., *Garrisons and Governments: Politics and the Military in New States*. San Francisco: Chandler, 1967.

Nasser, Gamal Abdel, *Egypt's Liberation*. Washington, D. C.: Public Affairs Press, 1955.

Union of Burma, Is Trust Vindicated? Rangoon: Government Printing Office, 1960.

Vatikiotis, P. J., *The Egyptian Army in Politics*. Bloomington: University of Indiana Press, 1961.

Wilson, D., *Politics in Thailand*. Ithaca, N. Y.: Cornell University Press, 1962.

VII

Ideology in the Developing Nations

One of the more interesting developments in the new nations has been the evolution of personal, party, and national ideologies. Usually syntheses of Western and indigenous elements, these new systems of thought are often found useful in achieving both individual and national political goals. This discussion will compare and categorize some facets of these ideologies, give several examples of environmental factors which form particular ideologies, assess the usefulness of ideology as a political tool, and analyze the place of ideology as a factor for national unity and stability.

Professed Political Ideologies

The efficacy of categorizing the great variety of ideological concepts which have appeared in the developing world may be questioned. The efforts of nationalist and political leaders to synthesize Western and native elements into unique syncretic concepts lends an air of exclusiveness to many of these patterns of thought. The multifaceted nature of some ideologies necessitates comparison on a variety of levels, thereby tending to fragment what may be a totality of thought. These objections are well-founded; yet, as long as these limitations are recognized, a gross categorization of selected variables may reveal certain similarities and help to systematize knowledge of the developing world. A final word of caution: this is a discussion of ideologies as expressed by their spokesmen, not of the realities which may contradict them.

In categorizing ideologies, it is necessary to make divisions on several levels. An analysis made on the basis of only one facet—say, the type of secular political system considered "best"—may neglect other important elements. The initial division is made on the basis of the overall secular political-economic system which governs the relationship between citizen and state. Five somewhat arbitrary categories, with illustrative examples, follow:

1. Individualist democracy
    Philippines
    Malaysia
    Liberia
2. Collective democracy
    India
    Cambodia
    Former French African colonies
    Ghana
    Mexico
3. Proletarian democracy
    Communist countries
4. Guided democracy
    Burma
    Pakistan
    Indonesia
    Egypt
5. Elitist
    Saudi Arabia
    Ethiopia

One preliminary generalization can be made: it is an obvious fact of political life in the postwar world that it is almost mandatory to profess an ultimate belief in democracy. Definitions of democracy and timing may differ, but the ideologies of almost all countries proclaim some sort of democratic system as the ultimate goal.

The variety of interpretations of democracy assembled below provide a fascinating example of how a term acceptable to almost all peoples may lead to misunderstanding through differences in use.

Regarding our own democracy, I initiated the idea, calling on the people to join to fight the diseases that were the results of free-fight liberalism. I called on the people to destroy free-fight liberalism completely, and to change it into Indonesian democracy, guided democracy, or democracy with leadership.

(Sukarno of Indonesia)

I would agree with my friend Julius Nyerere of Tanganyika . . . that the test of a democratic regime might not necessarily be the actual presence of a second party, or several parties, so much as whether or not the regime tolerated individuals. . . .

(Olympio of Togo)

The denial of fundamental human rights, the destruction of the rule of law, and the suppression of opposition have been brilliantly and felicitously rationalized. The outrageous declaration of an African leader that a one-party system is in accord with the democratic way of life has been ably defended by these spokesmen of the Western democracies.

(Awalowo of Nigeria)

. . . if there is any part of the world in which, if not democratic government in the Western sense but to use a phrase of Karl Popper's "open societies" or "open government" are possible, it is West Africa.

(Ayo Ogunsheye of Nigeria)

Broadly speaking, the African parliamentarian does not understand the meaning or function of the opposition. . . . He tends to regard the opposition as a saboteur who should be hounded out of the political arena.

(Chief Davies of Nigeria)

The state system—joint dictatorship of all revolutionary classes. The political structure—democratic centralism. This is New Democratic government; this is a republic of New Democracy. . . .

(Mao Tse-tung of China)

We must, therefore, have a democracy. . . . To my mind there are four prerequisites for the success of any democratic system in a country like Pakistan:

1. It should be simple to understand, easy to work, and cheap to sustain.
2. It should put to the voter only such questions as he can answer in the light of his own personal knowledge and understanding, without external prompting.
3. It should insure the effective participation of all citizens in the affairs of the country up to the level of their mental horizon and intellectual caliber.
4. It should be able to produce reasonably strong and stable governments.

(Ayub Khan of Pakistan)

The Democracy for which we rose in revolt on July 23 is a peaceful, clean democracy. . . . Its purpose is freedom of the individual, freedom of livelihood, true justice—individual freedom, collective freedom, a sound socialist society. . . . This is how we understand democracy.

(Nasser of Egypt)

A democracy is that form of government in which the majority runs things, where the majority means something, and the interests of that majority are protected; a democracy is that in which a man is assured of all his rights, not only the right to think freely, but also the right to know how to think. . . . A real democracy . . . in which not only the majority's rights prevail, but loaded weapons are handed to that majority!

(Castro of Cuba)

We do not conceive of democracy as simply a formal cover for an unjust social order. Hence, together with the guarantee of civil liberties to all Venezuelans, we propose the redistribution of national income . . . in a form that will make the economic misery of the majority of the people and social injustice disappear from the Venezuelan scene.

(Betancourt of Venezuela)

I consider the people who constitute a society or nation as the source of all authority in that nation; as free to transact their common concerns by any agent they think proper; to change these agents individually or the organization of them in form or function whenever they please.

(Jefferson of the United States)

A single country can, and has given rise to almost all these definitions of democracy. Herbert Feith, in his excellent political history of postindependence Indonesia, has analyzed the multiplicity of definitions present in that country at the time of independence. He notes that although support for democracy was universal, as was the complete absence of support for representative government and checks on the majority, there were a great number of interpretations of the term *democracy:*

In general, the parties wrote of democracy as "people's sovereignty," "peopleness" *(kerakjatan)*, *vox populi, vox Dei,* and "government of the people, by the people, and for the people." There were several references to the need for democracy in the social and economic field as well as the political, frequent affirmations of support for the equality of all citizens, denunciations of dictatorship, and declarations of support for such "basic rights of the people" as freedom of the press, freedom of assembly and demonstration, and freedom to strike. Moreover, the assumption was general that democracy implied parliament, parties, and elections. On the other hand, there was only one specific reference to majority rule and there were none to minority rights, the rights of individuals, or the institutionalized opposition. Only two parties associated democracy with law. Two other parties, the large PNI and the Catholic Party, declared their hostility to "liberalism."

Drawing on a wider range of contemporary views than the party platforms, one can see a great deal of variety in the prevailing image of democracy. Among one group of leaders there was a tendency to define democracy in terms of traditional political and moral ideas. This sometimes led to mystical definitions like that of Sutardjo Kartohadikusumo of PIR who asserted that democracy was "the unity of God with his servant" and President Sukarno's idea that "democracy is jointly formulating truth." Occasionally the symbol of democracy was attached to ideas of leadership as a lofty calling and of the true leader as a warden of the state and a spiritually superior being. And to many the symbol stood for a regeneration in modern form of the organically cohesive traditional community which had been disrupted by capitalist intrusions.

Others, by contrast, saw democracy as freeing individual men from the shackles of ossified hierarchical traditions, affording them opportunities to develop their personalities, and rewarding them on the basis of talent and achievement. This view was characteristic of Sjahrir and the young men of higher Western education associated with him in the Revolution, and it was also the view of a whole tradition of literary figures, most prominently the novelist Takdir Alisjahbana and the poet Chaeril Anwar. Some of the men with this image of democracy sought to establish its roots in indigenous social tradition. Thus they emphasized the egalitarian aspects of traditional village government and especially the idea of *musjawarah*, the notion that a leader should not act arbitrarily or impose his will, but rather make gentle suggestions of the path a community should follow, being careful always to consult all other participants fully and to take their views and feelings into consideration before delivering his syntheses-conclusions. Some of them argued further that the village had institutions through which protest could be channeled.[1]

Thus, Indonesia may be said to be the Afro-Asian world in microcosm.

1. INDIVIDUALIST DEMOCRACY. States in this category term themselves *democracies* and support economic and political individualism; thus it differs from Category 2, which might better be described as "social democratic." Two of the most prominent examples of Afro-Asian states with individualist democratic ideologies—Liberia and the Philippines—are both American-influenced, and have both developed relatively well-to-do economic-political elites with a stake in a semicapitalist ideology. Even in these states, however, the leaders do not speak in terms of stark individualism but in terms of the more socialized democracy now practiced in the United States.

Malaysia and the Philippines present an ideology more heavily private-enterprise conscious than even that of the United States.

[1] *The Decline of Constitutional Democracy in Indonesia* (Ithaca, N. Y.: Cornell University Press, 1962), pp. 39–40.

Emphasizing the necessity for establishing a "property-owning democracy," the ruling Alliance Party of Malaysia is less prone to support social welfare doctrines than the United States government is. In fact, Malaysian leaders often deny that their policies are based upon any ideology whatsoever. In the words of one politician:

> The Alliance Party, fortunately, has not tied itself up too much with ideology. To do so would have meant becoming dogmatic. Dogmatism is not good. Often dogmatism sacrifices pragmatism (practicalism). A combination of the two is preferable.[2]

Those states with nonsocialist ideologies appear to have several factors in common: their colonial experiences have not been such as to engender an emotional antiforeign attitude; the indigenous leadership is largely composed of the economic elite; and the economy of the nation has been relatively stable, thus staving off government control and strong opposition from political groups supporting other ideologies. This combination of factors is not common in the Afro-Asian world.

2. COLLECTIVE DEMOCRACY. Few of the emergent systems have not emphasized socialism as the necessary means of economic development and a natural concomitant to political democracy. Marxism in one form or another has had a tremendous impact on the thinking of Afro-Asian leaders. There is little acceptance of class war, democratic centralism, or other dogmatic elements of Marxism, but most would echo the words of the Burmese Revolutionary Council when it described "Our Belief":

> The Revolutionary Council of the Union of Burma does not believe that man will be set free from social evils as long as pernicious economic systems exist in which man exploits man and lives on the fat of such expropriation. The Council believes it to be possible only when exploitation of man by man is brought to an end and a socialist economy based on justice is established, only then can all people, irrespective of race or religion be emancipated from all social evils and set free from anxieties over food, clothing, and shelter and from inability to resist evil, for an empty stomach is not conducive to wholesome morality. . . .[3]

A number of countries cannot be described as purely individualist or collective; their policies either stress a mixed economy or are in

---

[2] *Malay Mail*, August 29, 1960.
[3] *The Burmese Way to Socialism*, Government of the Union of Burma, 1962, p. 1.

a state of change. It is not difficult to understand the interest in socialist doctrines: the paucity of developed resources and the lack of domestic capital makes capitalism appear questionable to political leaders, who present as evidence low per capita national income and foreign ownership of existing capital. This, they argue, leads to insufficient private capital accumulation. Thus, the state must take over the process of economic development. To the Afro-Asian socialist, Marxism appears to have a close relationship to the objective conditions of his world, although not to those of the West, where the rising standards of living have cut much of the ground out from under its theoretical foundation.

This type of thinking is buttressed by historical and environmental factors in the Afro-Asian world. Imperialism and capitalism have often been equated by nationalists desirous of eliminating all vestiges of foreign control. This antipathy is usually directed against foreign rather than domestic capital (often because the latter helps to finance the nationalist movements). This frequently emotional anti-imperialism-anti-capitalism may lead to postindependence laws and conditions designed to discourage foreign investors, resulting in an even greater dependence on hard-pressed domestic capital. Second, the colonial administration was usually paternalistic, controlling the economy in a manner less than conducive to free enterprise. Often, the administration owned transportation and communication media, set controls on exports, rigidly limited investment by other European nations, and—in general—established an environment which made state control after independence appear natural. Paradoxically, then, the capitalist colonial states prepared the way for the socialist ideologies that now prevail in their former colonies.

Some mention should also be made of the training of and influences on the nationalist leaders. Those who went abroad were often drawn to socialist groups, in part because of the greater interest in nationalist movements shown by left-wing organizations. Communists, Fabians, and socialists of all kinds greatly influenced the Afro-Asian student. Even those leaders who remained at home fell under the spell of the writings of various Marxists who damned imperialism and capitalism and appeared to provide a simple and easily understood theory to explain the relative poverty and social underdevelopment of Afro-Asia. Comparatively few nationalist leaders were unaffected by this thinking, and only after they had won control of their countries did their book-learned ideologies begin to require some serious revision. Still, socialism in its less doctrinaire form, vaguely calling for state action for the general welfare, has remained a simple ideology, easily understood by the masses. Finally, the postwar period has found the nations of Afro-Asia in a hurry, and socialism is considered a quicker road to economic development than capitalism is. Of course, the problem is that where national resources are few, as in Chad and Niger, or mismanaged as in Indonesia, no ideology is—in itself— going to bring the promised land.

3. PROLETARIAN DEMOCRACY. This comprises all shades of Communist ideology—Titoist, Trotskyist, Stalinist, Maoist, and so on. It also speaks in the name of both democracy and socialism, and often only the trained Marxist semanticist can discover the difference in the words used by both the Communists and the social democrats. The meaning is usually quite different, but the words themselves are not. When the Communists are in one of their united front phases, the words are even more similar—and for good reason.

Many of the same reasons which have brought individuals to support social democracy have been responsible for the further leftward turn to Communism. However, three factors need greater emphasis in the Communist case. First, the existence of the Soviet Union and Communist China as anticolonialist powers assures the Afro-Asian Communist outside support as well as a strong propaganda tool (European socialists have been disappointing to the more radical independence-minded nationalists). Also, the strong centralized organization of local Communist parties provides leadership and security to individuals disorganized by the changing societies of the developing world. It also allows the Communists to direct their ideas and policies more efficiently than other parties can. Perhaps most important, Communism appears to offer quick solutions to the individual or nation desiring to get ahead in a hurry. The totalitarian methods of Communism seem quicker than the give-and-take methods of democracy. It should be pointed out, however, that undiluted Communism appears to have gained comparatively few adherents in the Afro-Asian world. There is no legal Communist party in Africa and very few Communists, in spite of cries of anguish from many Western commentators. In the Middle East, only Israel allows a legal Communist party to exist. Where it has been successful in the Far East, Communism has hidden behind nationalism and what is called the two-stage revolution (the promise of initial tolerance to economic, social, and political groups, thus lulling possible opposition). Today, even those Communist parties supporting China in the Sino-Soviet dispute deny the validity of the commune system for their countries. Thus, where Communism has been victorious, it has depended upon nationalism and the un-fulfilled promise of democratic tolerance, both (according to Com-munist ideology) facets of "decadent" Western democracy.

4. GUIDED DEMOCRACY. This catch-all category includes those con-cepts which, while denying the possibilities of democracy today, promise some type of democratic system in the future. The "demo-cratic system," when defined, is usually not envisioned as a parlia-mentary government but as a limited democracy with strong leader-ship. There is little agreement as to the vehicle of transition, although in most areas the military plays a prominent role (Pakistan, Burma, Turkey, and others). In rare cases, this ideology is expressed by the civilian leader as, for example, Sukarno prior to his downfall. One of the classic theories of this development toward future "democracy" was that of Sun Yat-Sen, early revolutionary hero of Republican China, who envisioned three stages leading to a limited democracy. The best-articulated recent example of such a theory has been the "basic democracies" system of Ayub Khan of Pakistan, which is asserted to be a means of achieving democracy through training at lower levels and indirect elections of higher councils. Other examples abound, but few have been as systematically conceived as the two cited. More often, the period of tutelage remains indefinite and the system to be estab-lished vague.

Those who propound systems of "guided democracy" vary in their rationale for this combination of guidance and democracy. A few still pay lip service to Western democratic ideals but claim that the population is in need of training and education before these can be achieved. In the same vein, military men may claim that conditions in the country are not stable enough to allow the return to or the establishment of democracy. The Burmese military in 1958–60 and the former South Korean junta both argued in this fashion. More numerous are the examples of elites which deny the worth of Western democracy for their nations and which call for a combination of guidance and popular sovereignty. This sort of guided democracy may be in preparation, as in Burma, or almost complete, as in Pakistan. Its proponents claim it to be particularly well suited to the developing world where, they state, "liberal democracy" may lead to chaos and disunity but where the mores of the postwar period demand support for some sort of democratic system.

5. ELITIST SYSTEMS. Few leaders betray much sympathy for Western parliamentary democracy, at least in their own countries, but—to the extent that they express any ideology in a systematic form—fewer still deny the ultimate worth of the democratic system. Those who

do are normally members of right-wing minority groups such as are to be found in some parts of the Middle East, or spokesmen for traditional societies, such as Ibn Saud or the late Imman of Yemen. Category 5 then differs from the rest in that these elitists refuse to be associated, now or later, with any form of government which rests with the people. One individual or a chosen few can and should hold all power.

IDEOLOGICAL VARIABLES

Ideologies may be classed along nonpolitical lines. For example, a second level of classification is one considered a living issue in Asia, in parts of the Middle East, and in Latin America: the secular-religious dichotomy. Most new states refer in some way to a Supreme Being as an element in their view of life, but a few nations and several political parties consider a particular religion to be a vital part of the state's reason for being and its tenets a guideline for policy. Those states which believe a particular faith to have a central place in the national ideology include:

Burma (1961–62)	Libya
Thailand	Mauritania
Pakistan	Ethiopia
Saudi Arabia	Yemen

Other possible ideological variables center on such concepts as nationalism, racism, international commitments and methods of achieving goals.

Certain unique elements in a nation's ideology may be impossible to classify. They are part of the thinking of a people, formed of their history, their leadership, or their social setting. For example, Mexico's sad memories of past dictators has made the principle of no re-election an integral part of the national philosophy. Nkrumah's efforts to deify himself once made the person of the Osagyefo a central part of a philosophy which formerly consisted of little more than a desire for independence and a vague pan-Africanism. In India, Gandhi's asceticism and his wish to eliminate British rule made the virtue of the spinning wheel and a suspicion of modern machinery part of early Congress Party ideology.

Taking a cue from the works of Karl Mannheim, the next two sections deal with the sociology of knowledge of ideologies and efforts to use or distort them for political ends. The first point to be considered is that ideologies which gain influence over a nation do not spring full-blown into the minds of their spokesmen but develop as results of personal, social, and historical forces. Man himself and his thought result in large measure from environmental factors: i.e., the history of his nation, his personal background, the people who influenced him, his family patterns, and so on. Because he does not live in a vacuum, the spokesman for an ideology cannot divorce himself from the forces that have molded his people. Also, if the concepts he expresses are to have mass appeal, they must be identifiable by the people. Many an early Westernized intellectual has lost contact with the population by expounding ideas which have no relevance to his listeners. For example, former Indonesian Prime Minister (not elected) Sutan Sjahrir wrote in a manner instantly comprehensible to a western-educated intellectual, but he had little appeal among the Indonesian masses who could not understand his constant references to what are—to them—obscure Europeans. Therefore, if it is to influence a mass audience, an ideology must be oriented to its listeners. It is beyond the scope of this discussion to present studies in depth of the sociology of knowledge of each ideology in the developing world, or even thoroughly to analyze selected examples. Instead, an effort will be made to sketch the important elements in three illustrative cases: Sukarno's "guided democracy," Nu's religious state, and Ayub Khan's "basic democracy." These analyses serve only to illustrate the sources of ideologies and to point the way to deeper study. In each case, four environmental forces will be considered: historic, geographic and social, personal, and political.

THE SHAPING OF AN IDEOLOGY (I)
SUKARNO'S "GUIDED DEMOCRACY"

Sukarno, while still in power, was often described as being rather mercurial in his ideological associations—and, in fact, he prided himself on his ability to change. On two issues he has never wavered: his desire for a proud and independent Indonesia, and his ties to socialism. A third, and new, element is of particular interest: his unique potpourri of ideologies presented in various guises—"guided democracy," *Gotong-Rojong, mufakat,* and "a return to the Constitution of 1945." Since 1956, Sukarno has expressed his ideological beliefs in a series of slogans which stood for different Indonesian words and phrases. These included MANIPOL ("Political Manifesto"—Sukarno's speech of August 17, 1959), USDEK (the five basic elements of the Manifesto: "the 1945 Constitution, Indonesian Socialism, Guided Democracy, Guided Economy, and Indonesian Personality and Identity"), NASAKOM (the unity of Indonesia's three major groups—"National-ists, Religious, and Communists"), NASAKOM-MIL (the three major groups plus the military), and RESOPIM ("Revolution, Socialism, and Leadership"). As Arnold C. Brackman has noted in his history of Indonesian Communism, this barrage of slogans bore a striking resemblance to that of prewar China.[4] Behind these slogans were several basic facets of what Sukarno calls the National Ideology.

Pantja Sila. First, there is the original ideology of the independence period, the Pantja Sila or "Five Principles." These are five vaguely worded points emphasizing nationalism, internationalism, democracy, social justice, and belief in God. Articulated so generally as to be acceptable to all, these principles were the shield behind which all Indonesians could fight the revolution against the Dutch.

Unity. Sukarno continually stressed the need for national unity. His efforts to bring together nationalist, religious, and Communist factions now may appear naïve and even foolhardy to outside observers, but it was Sukarno's dream to create a single people—all seeking a greater Indonesia.

Guided democracy. "Guided democracy" called for guidance from above and a consensus achieved through discussion. Guidance and democracy are considered inseparable. In the words of Sukarno: "Democracy alone can defect to liberalism; guidance alone can defect to fascist dictatorship."

Return to the revolution or spirit of 1945. The revolution did not usher in a new Golden Age, and the next fifteen years brought the frustration of efforts to establish Western democracy and unity. Thus, the call went out from Sukarno for a return to the spirit of the revolu-tion and the original constitution, which had outlined a centralized system with strong executive powers:

> We are no second-rate nation, our Nation is Great, with Great Ambition, Great Ideals, Great Creative Power, and Great Tenacity. By returning to the 1945 Constitution, we have now rediscovered our Revolutionary Spirit, and achieved a *mental momentum,* which enables us to march forward quickly toward the achievement of another momentum in the field of overall construction and development, in order to realize the social-eco-nomic ideals of the Revolution.[5]

[4] *Indonesian Communism* (New York: Frederick A. Praeger, Inc., 1963), p. 267. For a discussion of the meaning of various words in the Indonesian political dic-tionary, see J. Van der Kroef, "An Indonesian Ideological Lexicon," *Asian Survey,* 2 (1962), 24–31.

[5] *Toward Freedom and the Dignity of Man,* Department of Foreign Affairs, Indonesia, 1961, p. 75.

Gotong-Rojong and mufakat. Sukarno considered coordination and cooperation the way to progress. This was probably the unique element in his ideology. In very general terms, he proclaimed: *"Gotong-Rojong* which is not static as is 'brotherhood' alone, but *Gotong-Rojong* which is dynamic, *Gotong-Rojong* with our sleeves rolled up, *Gotong-Rojong* 'One, two, three, heave!' *Ho lopis kuntul baris!"* In the political arena he was more explicit. Speaking of the United Nations but using Indonesia as his example, he told the delegates:

> Deliberations should be held in such a way that there is no contest between opposing points of view, no resolutions and counterresolutions, no taking of sides, but only a persistent effort to find common ground in solving a problem. From such deliberations there arises a concensus, a unanimity, which is more powerful than a resolution forced through by a majority of votes, a resolution perhaps not accepted, or perhaps resented, by the minority.[6]

What forces, then, influenced the formation of this ideology? Only some of the factors can be listed here, but these may lead to a more comprehensive view of an ideology in its own environment.

Historical factors.

1. The Indonesian revolution was a bitter and bloody one, leaving the idea of the revolution a highly emotional force in national life.

2. The nationalist movement was never able to unite for an extended period and thus was unable to present either a united leadership or a coherent program.

3. Indonesia's inability to achieve stable government under a parliamentary regime led to frustration and disappointment with western democracy.

4. The internal rebellions that racked the country in the post-independence years increased the desire for stable leadership and unity.

5. The army was never able to unite in order to present an alternative ideology.

Geographic and social factors.

1. Indonesia is composed of a wide variety of peoples with different languages, religions, and mores. This fact has led to a considerable emphasis on the idea of unity and coordination. (The national motto is "Unity in Diversity.")

[6] *Ibid.,* p. 142.

2. The village provides the rationale for and support of the idea of *mufakat*. As one Indonesian writer expressed it:

> All important elements within the village participate in a meeting (*musjawarat*), where all decisions are achieved not by majority rule, but by a process of talking things out until a common understanding is reached (*mufakat*) which is subsequently carried into effect under collective authority.[7]

3. The pattern of the Dutch colonial system, which was highly paternalistic, may have influenced the people to accept the idea of guidance.

Personal factors.

1. Sukarno was long influenced by things Indonesian and by a desire to synthesize these with Western concepts.

2. Sukarno was influenced by his experience in Communist states and by what he felt to be the advantages of unity and guidance within the Communist system.

3. Sukarno was never against a central place for himself and the 1945 Constitution provides him with that. He considered himself a father image, and the analogy of the family continually used in describing guided democracy fit in well with this concept.

Political factors.

1. Opposition parties were displaying dissatisfaction with Sukarno and his call for a return to the 1945 Constitution with its presidential rather than parliamentary system and support of "guided democracy" was a means of diminishing their power.

2. The 1945 constitution provided a rationale for his new powers.

3. New concepts kept the peoples' mind off the complexity of the nation's problems.

THE SHAPING OF AN IDEOLOGY (II)
U NU'S RELIGIOUS STATE

Former Burmese Prime Minister U Nu also emphasizes nationalism, socialism and unity, but gives his ideology special flavor by

---

[7] Soedjatmoko, "The Role of Political Parties in Indonesia," in P. Thayer (ed.), *Nationalism and Progress in Free Asia* (Baltimore: Johns Hopkins Press, 1956), p. 136.

his devout interest in religion, particularly Buddhism. No head of a
modern country has so expressly articulated the need for religion as
the cornerstone of a nation's growth and unity.

> Prime Minister U Nu is a man described by one Asian observer as "unique
> amongst the world's statesmen by his unparalleled piety and the embodi-
> ment of the ideal of Rajarsi, the ruler who is also a sage." Nu is termed a
> religious man even by his enemies, who, in fact, have at times blamed his
> interest in prayer, meditation, and religious questions for his weaknesses
> in administration. He has evidenced profound interest in furthering Bud-
> dhism and has used the machinery of the state to aid his cause. In his
> speeches, he has referred to his delight in religious activities and has
> publicly prayed for the "Back to Religion" movement. Nu has called for
> increased religious activity to unite a country torn by civil strife, at one
> time professing that "If we go to the root causes of the present disorders
> in this country, we will find that not less than 80 per cent of them are due
> to apathy to religion." At another time, he advanced the claim that "all
> activities directed towards the stability of the Union and the perpetuation
> of Independence are steps toward the propagation of the Sasana [religion]."
> Such statements find ready acceptance among the broad masses of the
> Burmese people.[8]

This interest in religion reached its zenith during U Nu's short-
lived return to power in 1960–62, when Burma established Buddhism
as the state religion but extended guarantees of religious freedom to
other faiths. The government agreed to aid Buddhist education, to
protect Buddhist shrines and works, and to strengthen Buddhist ways
and institutions. U Nu proclaimed the Buddhist state as the means by
which unity could be achieved in Burma; but shortly after its inauguration, fanatic religious leaders used it as an excuse for attacking other
faiths. A short time later, the second army coup put an end to the
constitution, and to the Buddhist state, although the army claimed to
be operating in a fashion compatible with Buddhist doctrine.

What forces have influenced this religious emphasis in Nu's ideology?

Historic factors.

1. Burma was not conquered until the end of the nineteenth century, and the memory of the monarchy and its relation to religion
remains strong.

2. Religion played a vital role in the prewar nationalist movement.

3. Although the country has suffered from religious friction, the

[8] F. R. von der Mehden, "Buddhism and Politics in Burma," *Antioch Review*,
XXI (Summer, 1961), 170.

religiously oriented feel that more—rather than less—religion is the answer.

Geographic and social factors.

1. Burma is a country somewhat isolated by nature. This isolation has helped to foster a more traditional perspective in dress, religion, and customs.

2. The Buddhist monk has been a powerful social and religious force in the village.

3. Burma has long held herself to be a center of Buddhist culture and religion.

4. The disgrace of being a colony after a glorious past turned the Burmese toward Buddhism as both a unifying and ego-enhancing factor. Many stated that merit gained in former lives was the reason that they were Burmese and not poor foreigners.

Personal factors.

1. U Nu is a devoutly religious individual who has expressed a deep concern for religious values ever since the 1930's. He has been known as "the monk politician."

2. A few of Nu's close associates have also been religiously and traditionally oriented.

3. The chaos of postwar Burma apparently strengthened Nu's feeling that a unifying force was needed and his background led him to regard religion as that force.

Political factors.

1. Some cynics have stated that Nu recognizes that religion is vitally important to the Burmese and has played upon that interest for political gain.

2. Religious interest groups, such as monks' organizations, and powerful religious leaders have long put pressure on the government to give more attention to religion.

3. The army had used religion as a tool against the Communists, and the country had been prepared for a greater interest in religion through army propaganda.

THE SHAPING OF AN IDEOLOGY (III)'
AYUB KHAN'S "BASIC DEMOCRACY"

The basic structure of Ayub Khan's ideology present and past is easier to depict than that of Nasser, Kasem, Abboud, or other military leaders of the Muslim world. His policies have been less ad hoc and he has been careful to explain his ideology to his people and to those outsiders who will listen. Here, too, there developed a certain frustration with earlier political processes and an attitude that the country's problems are unique. Three essential ingredients epitomize the ideology of Pakistan:

1. *Paternalism*. Ayub Khan's writings and speeches take the tone of a father talking to his children. His colleagues have publicly used this analogy.

2. *Frustration with the former "democratic" system*. Writing for an American audience, Ayub Khan once asserted:

> It is now the fashion to blame the politicians outright for this mess. Yes, they were guilty of many misdeeds of omission and commission; but there is one fundamental point in which I have a feeling they were rather sinned against than sinning. That is, they were given a system of government totally unsuited to the temper and climate of the country.[9]

3. *Eventual democracy*. A democratic system is to be formed, but only after preparation and only if it can fit the situation in Pakistan.

> We must, therefore, have democracy. The question then is: What type of democracy? The answer need not be sought in the theories and practices of other people alone. On the contrary, it must be found from within the book of Pakistan itself.[10]

Again, Pakistan's environment brought forward a different emphasis than that in Burma or Indonesia.

Historical factors.

1. The divorce of Pakistan from India left the country without an adequate civil service, thus making the success of any political system —particularly one with changing cabinets—questionable.

2. The country became independent on the basis of a religious ideal and the zeal of a few men. The most important of these men died soon afterward, and the religious ideals alone could not provide an adequate base for a modern state.

3. The political parties were unable to maintain unity or to agree upon a constitution or elections.

[9] "Pakistan Perspective," *Foreign Affairs*, 38 (July, 1960), 550.
[10] *Ibid.*, p. 551.

4. The colonial system, particularly in West Pakistan, prepared the way for a military takeover.

Geographic and social factors.

1. Pakistan is divided geographically; a weak parliamentary system could not keep unity.
2. Islam provides some basis for strongman rule.
3. The "basic democracy" which was established is somewhat similar to the former colonial system and therefore recognizable to the peasant.

Personal factors.

1. The Sandhurst training of Ayub Khan and some of his fellow officers led to an emphasis on efficiency and authority and to a turning away from tradition.
2. The chaos of civilian rule apparently had a considerable influence on Ayub Khan's personal views.

Political factors.

1. Some state that the slowness of the plan to develop democracy is a part of a clever device to maintain the army in power by promising but never delivering ultimate power.
2. Other military revolts may have influenced the army to try its luck in Pakistan. This was a period when a rash of army coups had occurred.

IDEOLOGY AS A POLITICAL TOOL

An ideology may be a sincere belief or a political tool, but it usually appears to be a combination of both. It is no enviable task to analyze a particular system of thought in order to ascertain when the spokesman is using it for political gain and when he is sincerely moved by his ideals. Since world leaders cannot be put on a psychiatrist's couch, their feelings must be deduced from their speeches and deeds and the comments of their intimates—weighed, perhaps, with a certain degree of cynicism. There is little doubt that ideologies have been consciously formed and articulated in order to achieve particular ends. A number of examples can easily be arrayed, although in each case evidence is circumstantial.

The idea of "guided democracy" and *mufakat* very effectively neutralized opposition political parties in Indonesia. In Burma, Nu's interest in religion and promise of a Buddhist state were emphasized by his colleagues to play upon the religious sympathies of the voter and to win the 1960 national elections. Nkrumah and other African leaders have employed the twin issues of nationalism and unity to strike at opposition politicians and parties. The dominant party of Mexico rides the horse of the Mexican Revolution and accuses opponents of being unsympathetic to that cause.

A more extended example may be useful in the case of Nasser. Neither the economic and social gains made under his leadership nor his sincere nationalism can be denied; nevertheless, it is possible to speculate on the political reasoning behind several elements of his ideology. One facet, the desirability of Arab unity, gives rise to the following possibilities:

1. It attracted attention away from internal problems. As one writer commented:

> It was clear that the campaign against "imperialism" . . . served a psychological as well as a political need: it turned the attention of Egyptians from their abiding problems to real and imaginary "enemies" at home and abroad, and gave them a new feeling of national pride.[11]

2. It could be used to diminish the old national fear of isolation.

3. It might be useful in gaining the inclusion of the oil-rich countries, such as Iraq and Saudi Arabia, thus aiding poorer Egypt.

4. It could lead to Egyptian hegemony over most of the Middle East.

In the use of ideology in the developing world, a crude pattern emerges to explain why ideologies have been considered politically useful. One or more of four factors normally can be the explanation for the political use of ideology.

1. It is helpful in eliminating or diminishing the power of the political opposition. This is particularly true when it stresses nationalism and unity.

2. It takes attention away from other embarrassing problems. Nationalism and imperialism are particularly useful here.

3. It lends legitimacy to primarily politically motivated acts.

4. It may allow the extension of power to areas outside the leader's immediate control. "Pan" movements of various types may be the best vehicle in this case.

[11] K. Wheelock, *Nasser's New Egypt* (New York: Frederick A. Praeger, Inc., 1960) p. 56.

New ideologies may be expected to appear in the developing world as reactions to new sets of problems, although their success in molding the minds of populations may be limited. The problems of mass communications in an underdeveloped country make indoctrination a particularly difficult task.

IDEOLOGY AS A FORCE FOR UNITY AND STABILITY

The usefulness of ideology in promoting unity and stability is obvious. If successful, it can be the catalyst necessary to amalgamate peoples of disparate backgrounds. Thus the period prior to independence saw efforts to unify the people under banners of *"Merdeka,"* "Self-Government Now," "Protect Religion," and so forth. The post-independence period has ushered in a whole host of new ideologies intended to strengthen the national government and/or party. These may be centered on one man (as in Egypt), based upon a return to past heritages (as in Indonesia and Burma), or based on an emphasis upon unity under the party (as in areas of former French Africa). One of the best examples of the formation of an ideology to establish unity is to be found in Communist China. During the takeover of China in the 1940's, Mao Tse-tung propounded the two-stage revolution. Under this system, political parties, some landowners, civil servants, and even capitalists would be allowed to exist in a limited pluralistic society. This promise made it easier to attract groups that might have been against the Communist revolution. It thus maintained unity while allowing the government to use the talents of the people. Meanwhile, "good" Communists were being trained. This stage of the revolution was short-lived, but it did provide a period of calm and unity in a most difficult time.

Modern ideologies successful enough to aid in the establishment of unity and stability normally should include several characteristics. The ideology ought to be general enough in scope and wording so as to unite a large part of the population. Doctrines that are too explicit may be difficult to fulfill and may not win mass allegiance. The very vagueness of the Pantja Sila in Indonesia helped to provide a degree of unity among conflicting groups during the revolution. Of course, a major problem may come when these general goals need some sort of detailed elucidation—a problem which religious nationalism, for example, encounters after independence. It is easy to gain the unity of Muslims or Buddhists against the Christian colonial power, but after independence frictions develop between secularists and sectarians and among the latter over the proper interpretation of dogma.

This is a major reason why national ideologies with a strong religious emphasis normally have not lasted long after independence, unless expressed in the most general terms.[12]

A second element usually found in successful ideological programs is the combination of ideology with organization. It is easy to understand why money and a central organization are essential in extending an ideology throughout the nation. Efforts by central governments to control all media of mass communication in the newly independent states are but a recognition of the importance of radio and newspapers in the developing world. Ideology may also help the organization by sugarcoating the more authoritarian aspects of central control.

An ideological campaign may fail if it is not accompanied by at least some long-term benefits or if the population is burdened with constant barrages of ever-changing doctrines. One explanation for the instability and disunity of contemporary Indonesia is that the country has been bombarded by so many different ideologies. And the failure of many newly independent governments to attain the goals expected of independence and democracy has been one of the factors responsible for the high rate of military coup in the developing world.

Finally, of course, when there is no consensus on basic goals or when sharp conflicts among different ideologies exist, disunity and instability result. This type of ideological conflict, with its concomitant chaotic conditions, is found in Vietnam, Indonesia, Iraq, South Africa, and Jordan, for example. The surprising fact is that relatively few Afro-Asian countries have really deep ideological frictions.

SELECTED BIBLIOGRAPHY

Almond, G. and J. Coleman, *The Politics of the Developing Areas.* Princeton, N. J.: Princeton University Press, 1960.

Anderson, C., F. von der Mehden and C. Young, *Issues of Political Development.* Englewood Cliffs, N. J.: Prentice-Hall, Inc., 1967.

Apter, D., *Ideology and Discontent.* New York: The Free Press, 1964.

Barnett, A. Doak, *Communist Strategies in Asia.* New York: Frederick A. Praeger, Inc., 1963.

Binder, L., *The Ideological Revolution in the Middle East.* New York: John Wiley & Sons, 1964.

[12] F. R. von der Mehden, *Religion and Nationalism in Southeast Asia* (Madison: University of Wisconsin Press, 1963).

————, *Religion and Politics in Pakistan*. Berkeley: University of California Press, 1961.

Butwell, Richard, *U Nu of Burma*. Stanford: Stanford University Press, 1963.

Davis, Harold E., *Latin American Social Thought Since Independence*. Washington, D. C.: University Press of Washington, D. C., 1961.

Emerson, Rupert, *From Empire to Nation*. Cambridge, Mass.: Harvard University Press, 1960.

Friedland, W. and C. Rosberg, ed., *African Socialism*. Stanford: Stanford University Press, 1964.

Huntington, S., *Political Order in Changing Societies*. New Haven: Yale University Press, 1968.

Legum, Colin, *Pan Africanism*. New York: Frederick A. Praeger, Inc., 1962.

Schwartz, Benjamin, *Chinese Communism and the Rise of Mao*. Cambridge, Mass.: Harvard University Press, 1951.

Sigmund, Paul E., Jr. (ed.), *The Ideologies of the Developing Nations*. New York: Frederick A. Praeger, Inc., 1963.

Vatikiotis, P. J., *The Egyptian Army in Politics*. Bloomington, Ind.: Indiana University Press, 1961.

VIII

CONCLUSION

As noted in the Introduction, political development in the developing world has not proceeded in the direction originally hoped for by early Western observers. Drawn largely from the earlier chapters of this book, an attempt will now be made to point up a few of the more important trends in the area under discussion. It should be noted that the developing world provides a great variety of political experiences. The trends analyzed below are by no means universal but only reflect what appear to be the dominant tendencies.

1. *While in most cases the institutions established out of the colonial period remain, the trend has been toward the development of political processes that have left these institutions with a primarily symbolic content.*

In Afro-Asia, there remain parliaments, courts, elections, and considerable paraphernalia attendant to democratic institutions gleaned from the former metropolitan powers of Western Europe. However, with the establishment of one-party systems, the increasing prominence of the military in civil affairs, and the decreasing role of political competition, Western institutions have tended to lose their original meaning. It should be noted that in all Afro-Asia only Ceylon and the Philippines have seen the national government thrown out and the opposition come into power by the democratic electoral process without a post-war coup. An equal rarity has been peaceful change of government at the state level, with India and Malaysia being the prime examples.

2. *The trend appears to be away from organized, legal political competition and perhaps even from party politics.*

Over half of the 56 new states of the post-war era now have political systems with no effective party activity or maintain a one-party pattern. We have also seen a growing number of polities making the transition from one-party systems to military control (for example, Algeria, Dahomey, Ghana, and Mali). Of the present military-dominated states of the developing world as a whole, fourteen had working party systems in 1960 while only four countries have gone in the other direction (the most prominent being Pakistan and South Korea, the latter going from civilian government to military and back to civilian within that period, while Pakistan's future is questionable).

Even Western democratic states such as India, Malaysia, Israel, and Singapore have found it necessary to put greater political restrictions on opponents as a result of perceived internal and external dangers to the nation.

3. *The military is becoming an increasingly important part of the decision-making apparatus of the new states.*

As pointed out in Chapter VI, the odds are now approximately 50–50 that a new state will have a successful military coup within the first decade of its independence. However, the prevalence of military coup is only one example of growing influence. Internal and external crises have increased the relevance of the military in civilian dominated states such as Israel and Lebanon, while the large number of coups must lead those governments still under civilian control to maintain a wary eye on the military in their own countries.

The entrance of the military into the political arena does not appear to be necessarily tied to any one colonial history or party system. Since 1958, military coups have materialized in former colonies of Britain, France, the Netherlands, Spain, Portugal, and Belgium, as well as numerous states that remained outside the formal control of Western colonial powers. In addition, coups have been directed against polities with no effective party systems (Thailand), one-party states (Ghana and Mali among others), one-party dominant states (Bolivia), two-party states (Honduras) and multi-party systems (Argentina, Brazil, and Nigeria among others).

4. *The trend appears to be toward longer periods in power for military regimes in the developing world.*

While the "caretaker" pattern of military control has not been eliminated in the developing world, as has been exemplified recently by Pakistan and South Korea, more lengthy periods of military rule are to be seen in all parts of the developing world. While a variety of uniquely national factors are responsible, partial responsibility must be given to the diminution of trust between military and civilian and the aforementioned decline in the support of democratic processes in the new states.

5. *Economically, the developing world is not holding its own with the developed states.*

A few simple statistics will suffice (and in the developing world few statistics are simple or accurate!) to support this statement. According to United Nations statistics:[1]

a) The developing world still depends upon primary products, and since 1960 there has been steady deterioration in its terms of trade as prices of industrial goods have gone upward and prices of primary products have shown a symmetrical tendency to decline.

b) The share of world trade of the developing nations has dropped from one quarter in 1954 to less than one fifth in 1966.

c) Whereas the United Nations Development Decade called for a yearly increase of at least 5 per cent in the GNP of the developing countries, it has only been 2–3 per cent owing to population growth and other factors.

d) Public debt in the developing countries has risen from ten billion dollars in 1955 to thirty-eight billion in 1965. Payment on public debt has arisen from one billion to three and one half billion dollars in the same period.

e) Foreign aid has dropped in the past fifteen years to significantly lower than the 1 per cent of GNP that the developing states were called upon to provide at the 1964 Geneva Conference (it was 0.72 per cent in 1965 and declining).

6. *In the political arena, perhaps the central factor hindering economic development still remains the dearth of qualified personnel at all levels of administration.*

Terms such as dictatorship, military domination, and mass party have tended to cloud over the fact that at the rural level the political situation is usually one of neglect, not domination. Not only has there been the continuing problem of insufficient qualified personnel (for which the colonial regimes can take a major part of the blame) but government tends not to reach the village level in a regular and meaningful fashion.

It would be remiss to conclude this survey without again providing some warning of what we *don't* know about the politics of the developing world. While there has been a vast increase in both discrete and

[1] United Nations, *Issues Before UNCTAD-II* (Geneva, Switzerland: UNCTAD, 1967).

general theoretical work in the field during the past decade, there remain vast gaps in basic areas of knowledge. In preparing this study, four primary problems in data were:

1) *Statistical accuracy:* Both political and economic statistics for the developing world often lack accuracy and it is difficult to judge the merit of the variety of national statistical offices. Most United Nations statistics are provided by the nation concerned without warning to the unsuspecting reader as to their veracity. While computerized systems for correlating data are to be found in many new states, the collection of the raw material at the local level remains of low quality and political factors often hinder an accurate or objective rendition of the results. Data are questionable for population, literacy, health standards, GNP, agricultural production, and election statistics.

2) *Country studies:* Descriptive country studies are at a premium, particularly for the new Afro-Asian states. While there may be research on specific elements of the new polities, we lack a significant number of works describing the total process and institutional pattern—and replication cross-nationally is rare. If the reader were to take the table of contents of any of a dozen American government texts, and, taking into account country differences, attempt to fill in our knowledge of comparable processes or institutions for most of the hundred states treated here, he would soon be discouraged by the dearth of information. Attempts are now being made by universities and some publishers to close this gap, but the long and frustrating efforts to replicate studies at the American state level are not encouraging.

3) *Communications between elite and mass:* Among more discrete studies a considerable amount of research needs to be initiated to assess more clearly the type and strength of lines of communication and organization between national elites and their supposed followers. As noted in this text, our own lack of precise information on this aspect of the mass party led to a serious misreading of the strength of Afro-Asian mass parties.

4) *Decision-making at the national level:* This is an extremely difficult area of investigation given the often closed nature of the process in the noncompetitive polities of the developing world. Perhaps one way of getting at this would be through the political biography, a system so well used by Richard Butwell in his study of U Nu of Burma. At any rate, this area of investigation is presently dominated by various forms of almost mystical "Kremlinology."

These are but a few of the multitude of research opportunities and problems to be found in the developing world. The author is reminded of a request made of him by the Fulbright Foundation of Burma in 1960 for a list of various topics in Burmese politics that would be fruitful for research. The only possible answer was to list the few examples of political science research that had been accomplished and then to note that the rest was substantially a *tabla rasa*.

APPENDIX

POLITICAL SUMMARY OF THE DEVELOPING NATIONS

Country	Mother Country	Date of Independence	Political Party System	Coups or Attempted Coups in the Postwar Period	Is Original Leader Still in Power?	Was the Struggle for Independence Violent? (Only Postwar cases)	Remarks
Afghanistan	—	—	Not effective	no	—	—	—
Algeria	France	1962	Not effective	yes	no	yes	Military coup overthrew original government
Argentina	Spain	1816	Not effective	yes		—	Recent action by the military makes the situation highly fluid
Barbados	U.K.	1966	Two-party	no	yes	no	—
Bhutan	—	—	Not effective	no			India still controls external policy
Botswana	U.K.	1966	One-party dominant	no	yes	no	—
Bolivia	Spain	1825	Multiparty	yes			Highly fluid political system
Brazil	Portugal	1822	Not effective	yes			Military has severely limited party activity
Burma	U.K.	1948	Not effective	yes	no	yes	Socialist-oriented military rule
Burundi	Mandate of Belgium	1962		yes	no	no	—
Cambodia	France	1953	One-party	yes	yes	minor	Prince Sihanouk dominates the political system
Cameroon	Mandate of France	1960	One-party	no	yes	no	—

Country	Colonial power	Date	Party system				Remarks
Central African Republic	France	1960	One-party	yes	—	no	—
Ceylon	U.K.	1948	Multiparty	minor	no	no	Rare case of peaceful party change
Chad	France	1960	One-party	no(?)	yes	no	Alleged coup to stifle opposition
Chile	Spain —	1818	Multiparty	no	—	—	—
China (Nat.)		—	One-party	yes	—	—	Political competition beginning to grow
China (Com.)	—		Proletariat	yes	—	—	Cultural Revolution makes situation fluid
Colombia	Spain	1810	Two-party	yes	—	—	Planned party exchange of power
Congo (Brazzaville)	France	1960	One-party	yes	no	no	—
Congo (Kinshasa)	Belgium	1960	Not effective	yes	no	yes	Military still remains prime decision-maker
Costa Rica	Spain	1848	Two-party	no	—	—	Other parties exist, but basically two-party
Cuba	Spain	1898	Proletariat	yes	yes	—	Castroism difficult to categorize
Cyprus	U.K.	1960	One-party dom.	yes	yes	immediate post-independence	Greek-Turkish division dominates party system
Dahomey	France	1960	Not effective	yes	no	no	Military action has limited political competition
Dominican Republic	Spain	1821	Multiparty	yes	—	—	—
Ecuador	Spain	1830	Temporarily not effective	yes	—	—	Military active in politics
Egypt	U.K. control	—	Not effective	yes	—	—	Abortive efforts at party organization

Country	Mother Country	Date of Independence	Political Party System	Coups or Attempted Coups in the Postwar Period	Is Original Leader Still in Power?	Was the Struggle for Independence Violent? (Only Postwar cases)	Remarks
El Salvador	Spain	1841	Multiparty	yes	—	—	—
Ethiopia	—	—	Not effective	yes	—	—	Remaining absolute monarchy
Gabon	France	1960	—	yes	no	no	—
Gambia	U.K.	1965	One-party dom.	no	yes	no	—
Ghana	U.K.	1957	Not effective	yes	no	no	Military now controls
Guatemala	Spain	1821	Multiparty	yes	—	no	—
Guinea	France	1858	One-party	no	yes	no	—
Guyana	U.K.	1966	Multiparty	yes	no	minor	Minor coup attempts of regional nature
Haiti	France	1804	Not effective	yes	—	—	Government now run unconstitutionally
Honduras	Spain	1838	Two-party	yes	—	—	—
India	U.K.	1947	One-party dom.	no	no	minor	—
Indonesia	Netherlands	1945–1949	Not effective	yes	no	yes	Military now dominates system
Iran	—	—	One-party dom.	yes	—	no	—
Iraq	U.K. Mandate	1932	Not effective	yes	no	no	Frequent changes of military regimes
Israel	U.K. Mandate	1945	Multiparty	no	no	yes	—
Ivory Coast	France	1960	One-party	no	yes	no	More stable and conservative of African regimes
Jamaica	U.K.	1962	Two-party	no	no	no	—
Jordan	U.K. Mandate	1946	Not effective	yes	no	no	Highly fluid situation

Kenya	U.K.	1963	One-party dom.	minor	yes	yes	—
Laos	France	1949	Not effective	yes	yes (?)	yes	Too unstable to categorize
Lebanon	French Mandate	1941–1945	Multiparty	yes	no	minor	Parties and politics oriented to religions and personality
Lesotho	U.K.	1966	One-party dom.	no	yes	no	Still too early to judge system
Liberia	U.S. sponsored	1822	One-party	minor	no	—	The True Whig Party in power for decades
Libya	Italy	1951	Not effective	minor	yes	no	Basically absolute monarchy
Malagasy	France	1960	—	no	yes	no	—
Malawi	U.K.	1966	One-party	no	yes	no	—
Malaysia	U.K.	1957–1963	One-party dom.	yes	yes	yes	United-front-type party in control
Mali	France	1960	Not effective	yes	no	no	Recent military coup
Mauritania	France	1960	One-party	no	yes	no	—
Mexico	Spain	1821	One-party dom.	no	no	—	Prototype of one-party dominant
Mongolia	Chinese and Soviet control	1921	Proletariat	no	no	minor	—
Morocco	France	1956	Not effective	no	no	yes	Monarchy remains powerful
Nepal	—	—	Not effective	minor	—	—	Monarchy still strong
Nicaragua	Spain	1838	Multiparty	yes	no	—	Could be termed multiparty undemocratic
Niger	France	1960	One-party	no	yes	no	—
Nigeria	U.K.	1960	Not effective	yes	no	no	Military dominates political system
North Korea	—	—	Proletariat	no(?)	yes	—	Multiparty façade
North Vietnam	France	1945–1954	Proletariat	no(?)	yes	yes	Multiparty façade

Country	Mother Country	Date of Independence	Political Party System	Coups or Attempted Coups in the Postwar Period	Is Original Leader Still in Power?	Was the Struggle for Independence Violent? (Only Postwar cases)	Remarks
Pakistan	U.K.	1947	One-party dom.	yes	no	no	Moving back to party government
Panama	Spain	1903	Not effective	yes	—	—	Recent military coup makes situation fluid
Paraguay	Spain	1811	Not effective	yes	—	—	Military rule makes parties ineffective
Peru	Spain	1823	Not effective	yes	—	—	Recent military coup makes situation fluid
Philippines	Spain-U.S. Mandate	1946	Two-party	yes	no	no	Rare competitive democracy
Rwanda	Belgium	1962	One-party	yes	no	no	Have been extraconstitutional changes
Saudi Arabia	—	—	Not effective	yes	no	no	Change starting slowly
Senegal	France	1960	One-party	no	yes	no	—
Sierra Leone	U.K.	1961	Not effective	yes	no	no	Military coup
Singapore	U.K.	1965	One-party dom.	minor	yes	no	—
Somalia	Italy-U.K.	1960	Multiparty	no	no	no	—
South Korea	—	—	One-party dom.	yes	no	no	Military left after elections
South Vietnam	France	1954	Multiparty	yes	no	yes	Fragile political system
Sudan	U.K. control	1956	Multiparty	yes	no	no	Parties returned after military rule
Swaziland	U.K.	1968	One-party dom.	no	yes	no	Still too early to judge type of system

	Colonial power	Date	Party system			minor	Continual military coups
Syria	French Mandate	1941–1945	Not effective	yes	no	no	Rare joining of two states
Tanzania	U.K.	1961–1963	One-party	yes	yes	—	Moving into party system on limited basis
Thailand	—	—	Not effective (?)	yes	—	no	Military coup
Togo	French Mandate	1960	Not effective	yes	no	no	—
Trinidad	U.K.	1962	Two-party	no	yes	no	—
Tunisia	France	1955	One-party	minor	yes	yes	—
Turkey	—	—	Multiparty	yes	—	—	Returned to party politics after military rule
Uganda	U.K.	1962	One-party dom.	minor	yes	no	—
Upper Volta	France	1960	Not effective	yes	no	no	Military coup
Uruguay	Spain	1825	Two-party	no	—	—	Government-welfare oriented
Venezuela	Spain	1811	Multiparty	yes	—	—	—
Western Samoa	U.K.	1962	Not effective	no	no	no	Elections primarily confined to matais or chiefs
Yemen	—	—	Not effective	yes	—	—	Civil war makes situation unstable
Zambia	U.K.	1964	One-party dom.	no	yes	no	—